Speak Lord, Your Servant Is Listening

Reflections on Faithful Communication in a Digital Age

Daniella Zsupan-Jerome

LITURGICAL PRESS
Collegeville, Minnesota

litpress.org

Printed in the United States of America.

Library of Congress Cataloging-in-Publication Data

Names: Zsupan-Jerome, Daniella, author.
Title: Speak Lord, your servant is listening : reflections on faithful communication in a digital age / Daniella Zsupan-Jerome.
Description: Collegeville, Minnesota : Liturgical Press, [2024] | Summary: "In Speak Lord, Your Servant Is Listening, pastoral theologian Daniella Zsupan-Jerome invites readers on a retreat-rooted in the Benedictine tradition-that promotes a spirituality of communication built on listening, engagement with the Word, and hospitality to others"—Provided by publisher.
Identifiers: LCCN 2024021278 (print) | LCCN 2024021279 (ebook) | ISBN 9780814689103 (trade paperback) | ISBN 9780814689110 (epub) | ISBN 9780814689622 (pdf)
Subjects: LCSH: Communication—Religious aspects—Catholic Church. | Church and mass media. | Internet—Social aspects.
Classification: LCC BX1795.C67 Z783 2024 (print) | LCC BX1795.C67 (ebook) | DDC 248.2—dc23/eng/20240610
LC record available at https://lccn.loc.gov/2024021278
LC ebook record available at https://lccn.loc.gov/2024021279

"Amid the fake news and the breaking news, the gossip, the memes, and the commentary that comprise so much of modern communications, Daniella Zsupan-Jerome has provided us all with the means of taking a deep breath. This book is a series of mini retreats for anyone in the communications business. By listening to God's Word and reflecting on how God communicates with us, Daniella invites us to reflect on how we communicate with each other."

— Greg Erlandson, former director of Catholic News Service

"This beautiful and necessary book shows us how to inject our increasingly divisive digital world with a sense of peace and hope, and it invites us to withdraw from the 24/7 connectivity now and then to interact with God so we may better interact with others."

— Mary DeTurris Poust, writer, communications specialist, and digital content creator

"A necessary addition to the growing library of communications spirituality! Encased in a monastic framework, these Scripture-based reflections on our digital culture challenge readers to consider intentionality in the digital experience and prayerfully reflect on whether communication encounters lead to authentic communion."

— Sr. Nancy Usselmann, FSP, director of Pauline Media Studies

"With this collection of timely and prayerful reflections, Dr. Zsupan-Jerome provides more than insight into a spiritual dilemma of our digital age. She offers a rehumanizing invitation to practice pausing, lingering with the word of God, and reorienting the way we communicate toward building up the Body of Christ. Imagine a world in which we more genuinely 'listen with the ear of our heart' and 'share our presence with one another.' That vision begins here."

— Samuel Rahberg, author of *Enduring Ministry: Toward a Lifetime of Christian Leadership*

"A kind word is better than the best gift."

Sirach 18:17, as quoted in the Rule of St. Benedict (31:14)

Gratitude

This project began in the spring of 2019 as a series of prayer reflections written to start each lesson for a semester-long class on Digital Media and Ministry. As I have continued to teach a class like this periodically ever since, I am continuing to grow in my conviction that creating solid contemplative spaces is necessary for accompanying our reflections on being faithful people in digital culture. As digital culture continues to evolve, contemplative spaces give us the opportunity to discern within this digital flow an ever more humane and faithful way forward.

I am grateful to the students who have prayed these reflections with me in these classes. I am also grateful for the wisdom and guidance of those who have inspired my exploration of contemplative work, especially Sr. Hélène Mercier, OSB. I am also deeply inspired by the good and faithful work of faith communicators in the media who have encouraged this book: Joe Towalski, Barb Simon-Johnson, and Greg Erlandson. Theirs is a ministry that deserves our support, prayer, and formation. Deep appreciation for the work of Fr. Paul Soukup, SJ, who, especially in his book *Out of Eden*, inspired the format of this book and has been a wonderful example of collegiality and scholarship in my career. Finally, to the Benedictines of

St. John's Abbey and St. Benedict's Monastery in Minnesota—for your witness, hospitality, and commitment to the Word—*Deo Gratias.*

Contents

Introduction

We Are All Communicators

When my son Gabriel was three years old, he loved going to church. Following the advice of Catholic mom bloggers, we boldly sat up in the front pews at Mass each week so he could see. It was amazing how much the ritual, the language, and the gestures of worship stuck with him and animated his play. At home, he laid out a "chalice" (stacking cup) and carried around a "Holy Gospel" (Dr. Seuss book) in solemn procession. He was awed by the cross, candles, and altar vessels. He gave "blessings" by dipping his fingers into any water he could find, including his drinking water, the dog's bowl, the bathtub, and, if it were not for my timely interception, the toilet. One day in the midst of an animated conversation with my husband, he came and stood between us and said, "Peace be with you." As any mother would, I pondered these things in my heart.

My younger daughter Lilibeth is that same age now. We still venture up front at church, now an even riskier move with two small children. The impact of the ritual on her faith, and how she participates in what is going on, is wholly distinct. Instead of the altar vessels and holy objects, it is the assembly's participation that has captured her spirit. She loves to sing, dance, clap, and move. I will never forget praying the Solemn Intercessions at the Good Friday liturgy last year. For Lilibeth, the occasion to stand and kneel ten times in a row was a delight.

More than just toddler sweetness, I believe that in these moments my children are offering something authentic and profound: they are *communicating* their faith. I have spent over a decade in professional theology, teaching women and men, lay, religious, and those to be ordained. In this context I have met many sorts of communicators of faith: bishops and theologians, teachers, evangelists, and preachers, Catholic media professionals and journalists: all communicators of the faith in one way or another. My husband has spent even more time in ministry work, serving as chaplain to the young and the old, both groups prophetic in their own ways. Yet our little children's first expressions of wonder and awe at the mysteries of our faith spoke the Good News to us anew. My little son marveled at things that have become part of the trappings of our Catholic life, and, let's be honest, have even collected dust. My little daughter illuminates the idea of full, conscious, and active participation in a whole new way. These moments with them feel like Easter morning, a new life, where Christ is alive and anything is possible.

As a Catholic theologian I am familiar with the content of our tradition. But my children have brought me a new joy and new life in their simple, faithful communication of what this tradition is beginning to mean to them. And so even after years of study and work in theology, I find myself saying again: *Speak Lord, your servant is listening.* And I sit with Eli in wonder as God speaks in his holy place to one little child after another (1 Sam 3:9-10).

The Call of Every Believer

I hope the reader will excuse this obvious outpouring of a parent's heart. I share about my children to offer a broader point. We are all, in one way or another, called to communicate our faith, and through that communication, to bring life and joy to others. This is no small calling. When we pause with this invitation, certain ministry professionals may quickly come to mind. We may think of bishops and the clergy who serve with them as teachers and preachers of the faith. We may picture church ministers, catechists, teachers, campus ministers, retreat leaders: all of whom aim to communicate faith in all sorts of settings. Catholic media professionals and journalists may also come to mind, as those who minister by informing, reporting, and reflecting on faith and life in public forums. And these days, we also must include the various prophets and preachers of digital culture who blog, vlog, post, and podcast the Good News to all the world. Indeed, many have responded to the risen Jesus' call to go and proclaim the Good News (Mark 16:15) by communicating the faith in these particular ministerial ways. We are blessed by their work, especially since the communication of the faith in public discourse can sometimes be challenging or negatively received.

As all these ministry professionals come to mind, do we also see ourselves in their company? The call to communicate faith is by no means exclusive to these "professional communicators" in ministry. In fact, the call is there for each believer. While some may indeed preach, teach, or evangelize, we often hear the Good News most clearly through everyday people of faith who seek to live fully and love God, while at the same time navigating the joys and struggles of daily life. Everyday believers with the capacity to invite others into their stories, their joys and struggles, offer a tremendous gift. Sometimes the most compelling lessons of faith emerge from the witness of such believers, who both claim and can generously share their stories. Communicating our faith is self-gift, a way of laying down our lives for the building up of others. Our faith calls us all to grow into our capacity for such self-gift. We each are called to be ready to give a reason for our hope (1 Pet 3:15). And we do this best through authentic, meaningful, and honest communication about things that matter.

In this digital age, we very often navigate the joys and struggles of life while gazing at the screen and scrolling or tapping away. We see so much wonder. There are images of love, families growing, generosity, and compassion. There are comments that encourage, support, and praise. There are articles and clips that expand our minds and spark the imagination. We also see brokenness. Ugly comments, mean-spirited content, vitriol, hate, falsehood, time-sucking clickbait, content that leads endlessly to nowhere. Especially at this time in our history, telling our stories generously and authentically really matters. But we may wonder: *In this shifting, intense world of digital media, how do I share on the screen who Jesus Christ is in my everyday life?*

We may again be quick to jump to the examples of "professionals" as we reflect on this. Social media influencers and digital evangelists have made a significant commitment to cultivating their presence and network on digital platforms. God willing, their good work helps to make present the Good

News and reveal Jesus Christ in digital culture. Yet the call of the believer to communicate faith, whether in digital spaces or elsewhere, is much more fundamental, and happens in countless ordinary ways. We do not need to be "specialists" to communicate faith. Parents teaching prayers to a child communicate faith. A couple having a meaningful conversation about their lives, their faith and hopes, communicate faith. Co-workers or neighbors offering encouragement and help to one another communicate faith. Longtime friends counseling each other in moments of crisis communicate faith. A cashier, driver, office receptionist, or delivery person who serves the public with love, joy, peace, patience, kindness, goodness, faithfulness, gentleness, and self-control, communicates faith.

Those familiar with the New Testament will recognize these qualities as the fruits of the Spirit, listed in Paul's Letter to the Galatians (5:22-23). These qualities are markers of a self-giving, generous person. For the Christian, these are also signs that a person is following the guidance of God's Spirit in life's everyday moments. It is in these everyday moments, most often through the way we relate with one another, that we are given the opportunity to communicate the Good News of Jesus Christ.

From Communication to Communion

Communicating the faith matters, and it is a call for all of us. The story of God's love over time holds each of us and also calls us forth to claim and tell our stories. For the believer, this begins with deepening one's awareness of the presence of God.

Out of that awareness, we share the Good News of God's presence with others, becoming community along the way. The disciples who walked with the risen Lord on the road to Emmaus, and who recognized him in the breaking of the bread, teach us this lesson. Recognizing at once the presence of Christ with them, this awareness moved them. Hearts on fire, they ran to tell others the Good News of their encounter. This is faith communication: to live out of authentic encounter with the Living God and to let this encounter move us more deeply in relationship with others.

The great theologian Cardinal Avery Dulles once said that "the Church is communications." Integral to who we are as believers is our call to gather toward communion with God and one another. Communication, especially of our shared story of faith, is integral to this. When we communicate, we share of ourselves and learn to receive the gift of another. Through communication we build relationships and sustain communities. When it comes to communicating faith, this becomes both a way and an expression of our communion. The call into this dynamic is for every believer, from ministerial leaders and theologians to everyday believers, and even to joyful and energetic toddlers during Mass!

When my small children began to express the impact of the Mass on them in their unique and playful ways, they were living into this same fundamental call. Expressing their faith in movement and play, they invited those of us around them into a holy communication space as well, witnessing divine mystery in dialogue with innocent human joy. My recollections of this, shared here with readers of this book, now expand their joyful faith communication even further. These small acts of genuine self-expression become gifts when they deepen life and meaning for others. Such communication also invites participation. Witnessing a story compels us to storytelling as well.

Living in a time when communication (and its technologies) has deeply shaped our culture, each of us is faced with the opportunity to reflect on how our communication connects us to God, our faith, and one another. This is not just a social opportunity but rather a deeply spiritual one. What is communication, this human social ability that connects us to one another, and how might we be more intentional about practicing it toward wholeness and holiness?

From a faith perspective, there is a profound invitation here for every believer to consider social communication as a practice of faith. Imagine our conversations, from simple interactions to formal public discourse, if we reframe communication not as content exchange but as encounter, human and divine. This book is an invitation to every believer toward reframing and reclaiming communication as a fundamentally holy practice. In our digital age, this invitation also calls us into a prophetic role.

Communicating Faith in the Digital Context: A Person-Centered Approach

In our day and time, using the internet and engaging on social media is an everyday habit for the majority of American adults. Perhaps you have thought about how to bring your faith into your presence and activity in digital spaces. To approach digital culture from the perspective of faith, it is helpful to reflect on our basic assumptions about digital spaces. Our experience of digital culture is heavily shaped by engaging with technology in the form of the latest tools, gadgets, software, applications, and platforms. In some ways, technology frames the digital spaces we inhabit. Yet even though we experience digital spaces through screens on gadgets, we are ultimately connecting with *other people* and engaging in interpersonal communication. This is a fundamental truth, and one that is essential for bringing our faith to the digital experience. It is also a truth we can easily forget, especially when all we see is pixelated text or images on a screen. Our broader access to generative AI (artificial intelligence) has also muddled our sense of where (or whom) the content on our screens comes from. As Pope Francis reflected some years ago about the digital world, it is a network not of wires but of people.[1] This wisdom endures today. The screen mediates our presence, but it is still human presence, yours and mine, that populates the digital realm.

Another big question for every believer is this: What, or better, *who* else ultimately animates or gives life to the way we connect with one another through digital communication? In the Christian tradition, the Holy Spirit is closely connected to our beliefs about communicating faith and how this builds

[1] Pope Francis, "Communication at the Service of an Authentic Culture of Encounter: Message for the 48th World Communications Day," January 24, 2014.

community. We might recall the Spirit at Pentecost giving the ability to speak, inspiring the preaching of the Gospel, reminding the disciples of the Word of God, and guiding them into all truth. Is it proper to think about the presence of God's Spirit moving through the digital network, where not only two or three but millions are gathered? The Spirit is our Counselor, the Advocate, the breath of God who makes God's Word manifest. Yes, it is true that technology, the work of human hands, makes digital communication possible. But wherever there is life, flourishing, creativity, and dynamism, God is the author. I believe that God's Spirit animates our interactions in digital spaces just as much as the Spirit animates our face-to-face interactions, guiding us to faithfulness in both contexts. In step with the Spirit, how can we communicate faithfully, as true disciples, as we encounter one another online?

We are living in a world where anyone with an electronic gadget and access to the internet can also share their life on the screen. Since the COVID-19 pandemic in 2020, it is even more clear how much our lives depend on these technologies. The boundary between online and offline has indeed become porous and blurred; these days we are living "onlife."[2] Through constant connectivity, our lives partially unfold in digital spaces. To these spaces we bring our interactions, our sharing of thoughts and reflections, our desire for exploration and learning, our creativity, and our hopes, joys, and spirit. Digital

[2] Dicastery for Communication, "Towards Full Presence: A Pastoral Reflection on Engagement with Social Media," May 28, 2023, paragraph 9.

spaces like social media platforms or comment feeds under specific content are animated by our human spirit and presence. We are inhabiting these contexts by bringing and sharing who we are in them. This of course includes our faith, the core of who we are and how we make sense of the world.

If we hold fast to the assumption that it is not so much content but rather people who populate digital culture, from the perspective of faith, a person-centered approach really matters. When I began my research about digital culture and communication over a decade ago, I came across an example that illustrates this truth, and it still works well today: finding recipes online. When the internet became widely accessible in the 1990s, people could find a recipe online on a website like foodnetwork.com that looked almost identical to a page in a cookbook. The ingredients were there, the directions were there, and, because it was on a website, perhaps some other flourishes decorated the page. Fast forward a few years to the 2010s: on the same website one could still find a recipe, just like in a cookbook. What was remarkably different was the number of user-generated comments underneath the recipe that both animated and filled out the story of a particular dish. People's comments added presence, community, and perhaps a touch of authenticity to the recipe. Fast forward to today: the story of the online recipe continues to change. These days, influencers and bloggers narrate the story of a dish for several paragraphs before disclosing the ingredients and preparation process at the bottom of the page. The recipe now finds itself told in the format of storytelling, re-presented as a practical detail in a broader narrative. This format makes room for advertisers on the page, who compete for our attention while we scroll to the bottom. The presence of an audience engaging with the story of the recipe is so assumed and valued in these digital spaces that it has become something from which to profit. Bloggers and influencers monetize the presence of readers who come to engage with their content. As digital culture evolves with the impact of generative AI, the swift availability of tailor-made recipes or menus still depends on the big data of collective recipe wisdom that this technology can rapidly aggregate.

Faithful Communication: Rising to the Challenge

People connected to one another remains the essence of digital culture even as our technologies become more advanced. We are living in a networked way, bringing our presence to both digital and face-to-face spaces. Adapting to this massive cultural shift has become the water we swim in, especially in the past few decades. How do we as people of faith navigate these waters? Digital culture has been impactful for the life of faith and raises a unique set of challenges, especially around communication. For one, advances in social communication have leveled the field of who gets to speak their mind to the world, whether the topic is politics, lifestyle, health, parenting, work, or indeed, religious faith. In a digital age, we can all communicate publicly about our faith and do so in a variety of ways. Some people post inspirational images, videos, or stories. Some share food for thought and scholarly analysis. Some gather or share prayer intentions. Some report on the life of the church in the world. In addition to these ways of interacting, many of us wade into the unpredictable waters of comment feeds and engage in exchanges that can inspire, encourage, challenge, anger, or frustrate. More so than content-sharing, it is the comment feed that can really test our ability to communicate what we believe with the same fruits of the Spirit listed above.

Another unique challenge is that of discernment. With the immense amount of content that is available to us in the digital realm, how do we discern what is good and truthful information about the faith? By what criteria can we receive faith communication and judge it to be authentic and edifying? How can we make prudent decisions about what is good content to pass along to others? In the digital age, this is a new and increasingly important faith communication skill to develop.

Digital culture is built on communication. In this context, our own approach to communication as people of faith is fundamental. When discerning our digital presence, we are called to think and pray about *how* we share our faith. While many of us may not explicitly communicate *about* the faith, such as through catechetical explanations or theological articles, we are still conveying our faith through our *manner* of communication. For example, sharing the Pope's latest teaching or a report about his pastoral activity is a straightforward way of communicating about the faith. Engaging in the comment feed under that same posting in a loving, kind, honest, generous manner, especially among critical voices, is also an act of communication that expresses faith. Here is an important distinction between *communicating about the faith* and *faithful communicating.* Communicating about the faith is focused more on sharing content: the truth of the faith manifest in its teachings and practices. Faithful communication, on the other hand, is focused more on the relational dimension: to share oneself authentically, modeled on Jesus in the manner of our lives.

An important caveat is that communication about faith and faithful communication are in no way in opposition. The distinction I am making here is about how one can communicate *about the faith* through the sharing of specific faith-related content, or how one can communicate faithfully by bringing a *faithful presence* to a digital space that demonstrates one's belief in the Gospel and bears the fruits of the Holy Spirit. Ideally, one can do both. But the distinction is helpful because faithful communication, achieved through our interactions and presence, is something I believe every Christian is called to at all times, regardless of the topic being discussed.

Faithful communication is about sharing our presence with one another, whether face-to-face or in mediated ways. Regardless of the medium, communication remains a relational activity integral to being human. Communication begins even before a child is born, in a mysterious, wordless but incarnate way between the mother and her child in the womb. I will forever remember the experience of being pregnant with my children, going for checkups, and hearing their strong, galloping heartbeats through the fetal heartbeat monitor. What a profound sense of their presence those moments brought me. More than the positive pregnancy test, more than the doctor's confirmation, more than the physical changes to my body, it was the act of listening and hearing these fast *thu-thumps* through the fetal monitor that first revealed their presence to me. Communication is deeply part of who we are, how we relate to one another, and how we find meaning in the world.

Faithful communication likewise is an integral human quality. Through the way we relate to one another, we convey something about what is ultimately meaningful for us, what our values are, how we make sense of the world. The manner of our communication is a witness to this internal reality. Every human person shares in this ability to witness, regardless of age, language, literacy, skill, or training. This ability to witness is a feature of our God-given dignity and the fact that we are made in God's image and likeness. We are made in the likeness of a loving, relational, communicative God, and we express this likeness in turn when we love, relate, and communicate. This is why it is both heartwarming and profound to see how my toddler children are beginning to express their faith, each in their own unique way. They are living into their God-given identity by expressing in word, play, movement, and gesture what is meaningful to them.

Recently, my son asked me to record a video of him playing with and explaining his favorite toys: his plastic counting blocks based on the children's program Numberblocks. He did this after some months of viewing other people's fan-made videos of Numberblocks online. For him, after viewing the show, playing with the blocks, and viewing fan-made videos, this was the natural next step of communicating his deep interest in the children's program. In a digital world, he is absorbing the manner and style of communication people exhibit about their interests and wants to replicate it. The result was a five-minute video he narrated with ease in the style of a young influencer. All of this without any coaching from me or his dad.

Digital culture and communication are deeply influential and formative for how we are living in the world. Our technologies have built digital culture, and now the digital culture is shaping us. Faithful communication has a prophetic call in this dynamic. From the perspective of faith, we know communication remains a profoundly human act, full of faith and spirit, and integral to who we are and how we relate with one another. How do we ensure that these deep values continue to abide in and give life to our communication practices in the digital realm? What values about faith, presence, and spirit will our children absorb as they grow up in a digital world? What manner of faith communication will they grow into? These questions are worth our attention as people of faith.

Prayerful Communication

If faithful communication is integral to who we are, and if it has a prophetic role for shaping digital culture, it is indeed worth our attention and our reflection. Here is an invitation to think about communication *prayerfully*, even as a holy practice. At first, praying with the idea of communication might seem a little unusual. When it comes to themes or topics we as Christians pray about, the spiritual tradition offers us plenty. The liturgy and the liturgical year, for example, invite us into regular seasons of repentance, introspection, anticipation, and celebration. Events of life, such as births, milestone achievements, forks in the road, failures, illness, and death all lead us to wonder about deeper meaning. We may have a devotional life that prompts reflective prayer in the company of saintly figures or through certain prayers or rituals. Within all of this, we may wonder how the integral human activity of communication may fit in as an occasion, in and of itself, for reflective prayer.

As we have seen, communication is a basic human activity, part of our nature, like breathing and eating and drinking and sleeping. Can these basic activities evoke wonder and mystery? Do they reveal the presence of God? Is there deeper meaning held in the way we relate with one another through word, gesture, and silence? Can we communicate as a holy practice? I would propose "yes" to all of this, but first with the invitation to pause long enough to begin to make these discoveries. Without an intentional pause, our basic human activities are mere signs of the mundane.

Many monastic communities practice what is called *statio*, Latin for "standing." During *statio*, members of the community line up and stand quietly for several minutes before entering their chapel or worship space for liturgy. During this time, they bring their attention to the present moment, and focus their awareness on the here and now. This pause is time that opens the ear of their hearts[3] and helps them enter more

[3] The phrase "ear of the heart" has its origin in the Rule of St. Benedict, which begins: "Listen carefully, my son, to the master's instructions, and attend to them with the ear of your heart" (Prol 1).

deeply into their shared prayer with God and one another. *Statio*, in contemporary spiritual language, is a mindfulness practice. It is standing still in the moment so the moment is not lost on us. In such standing still, we may actually discover the mystery that is already present, the breath that is already giving us life. Standing still, the mundane and the obvious reveal their grace.

Thinking prayerfully about communication is like a *statio*, a mindfulness practice. Communication is something we already do through the range of abilities each of us has to relate with what is around us. The prayerful moments provided within this book will invite us to stand still, to be mindful about how and toward what end we engage in these practices, especially as faithful communicators. Focusing on the way we relate to God and one another as our most fundamental form of communication, faithful communication calls us to listening, mutuality, presence, and more.

The Christian spiritual tradition has wisdom to share here, not only in content but in the various practices we inherit that are, in essence, expressions of faith communication. The monastic tradition, for example, offers invaluable wisdom on how to enable faithful people to love Christ and live well in community. Central to monastic wisdom is intentional, healthy, measured communication. The platforms of our interactions may have changed since the days of early monastics, but our call is the same. We are still seeking wisdom on how to relate faithfully with others and be a community rooted in the Word and centered on Christ. Faithfulness to Christ and living well with others defines a solid standard for digital culture and communication. And the invitation to be rooted in the Word takes on a whole new meaning in our time, when we experience a constant flow of words through the screens of our electronic devices. How might we find meaning, stability, and community in a time such as ours?

Being prayerfully attentive to our communication, we might discover a deeper spirituality that holds wisdom for such contemporary questions. Living at a time in history when communication technologies have radically redefined society and culture in the time span of decades, we may wonder about both the power and limits of human communication. Where is God in all of this? Quite close. Christian theology holds that communication is not only integral to being human, but it also describes for us something essential about who God is. Christians believe communication to be a lens for understanding who God is and how God relates with creation and with humankind. God's communication throughout it all is much more than just the exchange of ideas or information. More properly, God's communication is a gift of self, offered in love.[4]

We believe in a God who communicates. This elevates the meaning of human communication from an interpersonal act to a theological one. Our communication is rooted in God's image and likeness. Like God's communication, the ultimate expression of our communication is that of loving self-gift. This means that our communication first and foremost grows

[4] Pastoral Instruction *Communio et Progressio* (On the Means of Social Communication), 1971, no. 11.

from our spirituality, our communication with God. Out of this inner relationship, communication forms a bridge to how we relate with others as well. If we communicate well, we make a gift of ourselves and open ourselves to the gift of the other. The bond created, when rooted in Christ, is the very bond of community. Appreciating the value of communication for self and for others, the Christian spiritual tradition over time has placed good emphasis on communicative acts like listening, keeping silence, and encountering the living Word of God through various prayer practices.

Spiritual Skills for Digital Culture

Discerning faithful communication, especially in our digital culture, can draw deeply from the wisdom of Christian spirituality. For example, esteeming silence, practicing listening, discerning wisely, and cultivating attentiveness and presence are prophetic practices for today's busy, noisy world.

Our relationship with silence in digital culture is rather complicated. We are overwhelmed by the noise and constant chatter of the digital world, but we also struggle with disengaging from it by putting our devices away. The proliferation of electronic gadgets and the constant flow of information we experience through them is both a cause and a symptom of our lack of silence. In contrast, silence affords us the necessary time and space for making our communication intentional. In our digital culture, re-embracing silence as part of the pattern of communication is integral for relating more intentionally, thoughtfully, and humanely with others. Without the time and space to reflect, our utterances are reduced to impulsive reactions and are mostly about us paddling to stay afloat in the deep sea of information. This kind of reactive communication is mere cognitive survival, rather than the deeply human, relational act that builds social bonds. Carving out silence remedies this impulsive posture. In silence and solitude, we find the space to orient ourselves properly to God, self, and others. Silence helps to make communication a holy practice.

Prioritizing listening is also especially prophetic for digital culture. Listening is not just an interpersonal skill. It is a spiritual disposition, a state of being open and receptive to what is beyond us, which is ultimately God's Word. It is a hospitality of the heart, that center of our being where we encounter God. The ability to listen, to open the ear of our hearts, is neither easy nor automatic. It takes some work and discipline. Part of the challenge is cultivating stillness and esteeming silence so we *can* listen.

Another part of the challenge is discernment: understanding and trusting what we are listening *to*. Assessing information well and discerning the source of the words we allow into our hearts is an important skill for digital culture. We hear plenty from others as we encounter a constant flow of information through our devices. Discerning the words we receive is not only a practical but a spiritual skill, a kind of *spiritual literacy* especially needed in our world of constant connectivity. In our digital age, where media literacy is already a skill we recognize as useful, this spiritual literacy is emerging as another necessary ability, not only to understand but to discern the spirit of the content we come across.

In the same vein as listening, digital culture also poses the challenge of presence and attentiveness. Because of the ubiquity of our electronic devices, we can be simultaneously present and absent, oblivious to our physical location while paying attention to our screens. Furthermore, what we are paying attention to on the screen is usually multilayered or diffused between several windows. From the perspective of spirituality, where presence and attentiveness are deeply held values, such a diffusion and separation of our attention from our physical setting is concerning. As the late Benedictine monk Terrence Kardong has observed: "It seems to me that the phenomenon of a bunch of people all talking on their cell phones instead of to one another is really kind of a foretaste of hell, or at least purgatory. Everybody is talking but nobody is actually present to the person in front of them."[5] While connectivity at our fingertips brings many blessings, Kardong's wise warning highlights how integral presence and attentiveness are to building and sustaining good relationships. Appreciating this point, an emerging challenge in digital culture is how to sustain this humane, relational presence whether we are communicating face-to-face or through screens. Can a sense of stability or rootedness shape the spirit of digital encounters and digital spaces? This too can be a holy practice.

Communication connects us with God and with one another. Praying with and about our communication is all the more important today, in a culture defined by rapidly changing

[5] Terrence Kardong, OSB, *Conversation with Saint Benedict: The Rule in Today's World* (Collegeville, MN: Liturgical Press, 2012), 91.

communication technologies. My toddlers are growing up in a world of video chats, "asking the internet" any question at any time, and expecting Alexa to respond to their voices. Information technologies are everywhere around them. I sometimes wonder whether in their young minds, communication is simply something these powerful technologies do, rather than the profound and sacred human ability moving us toward communion. With the explosion of accessible artificial intelligence tools for composition, writing, and creativity, I wonder all the more about the importance of rooting communication more deeply in this spiritual soil.

Our Approach: *Statio*, Listen, Reflect, Ponder, Pray

Whether you are a person of faith who is interested in being more intentional about your presence in digital spaces, or you engage in faith communication as a vocation or ministry, this book invites you to prayerful reflection about communication as a holy practice. We can communicate our faith because God's Word has addressed us first. This book invites us back to the Word, specifically the Word of Scripture, to learn about the communication of the faith from within its stories. Scripture is full of lessons about faithfulness and right relationship with God. But what does it reveal to us about communication itself? What can we learn therein about how God communicates and how we are called to faithful, authentic communication in turn? What can Scripture teach us about communicating our faith, whether in our families and communities, in a professional capacity, or through the vast public landscape of digital culture? Through twenty Scripture stories, you are invited to *experience* the Divine Word addressing you, communicating with you as you contemplate these passages. You are invited to listen to each one with the ear of your heart, encounter the living Word, reflect on what it reveals to you about communication, and pray about how this speaks to your life and vocation.

In this way, *Speak Lord* invites us on a retreat. Taking a retreat is a longstanding spiritual practice. A retreat is movement to a quiet space to better focus on our interior lives, a desert place where we can listen, be still, and grow in awareness of God. For most of us, living in these busy, hectic days of the twenty-first century, this is a refreshing invitation. At the same time, like the desert monastics of the third century, retreating can also call one into the wilderness, to a place of sorting out tough questions, wrestling with temptations, and learning to sit with oneself in peace. By inviting us into the wisdom of Scripture, this book strives to create a space for both: resting in God, but also wrestling with meaningful and complex questions about what it means to be a faithful communicator today.

As an invitation to retreat, the structure of *Speak Lord* is modeled loosely on the ancient monastic prayer practice of *lectio divina*. *Lectio divina*, or holy reading, is a contemplative practice that seeks the living Word of God in Scripture. Through the method of this practice, *Speak Lord* invites us into a contemplative space where we can slowly and prayerfully encounter God's Word. This is a prayer practice that is about meeting God, allowing God to address us, and resting in God in the experience. Rather than scholarly biblical analysis, *lectio divina* is soul-space for discovering who we are in God. In this sense it is a deeply formative practice in which we enter into God's communication. From this we grow into our identity as people of faith, communicating our joys and hopes in the world.

The book can serve as the backbone of an actual retreat or simply as a spiritual resource for your regular devotional life. No matter the context, each reflection proposes a structure that moves us along in prayer on the following path: *Statio*, Listen, Reflect, Ponder, and Pray.

We begin with a basic disposition of attentiveness called "*Statio*." As discussed above, *statio* is a monastic term for taking a holy pause, for standing still long enough to become attentive and present to the moment before us. This moment of standing still allows us time and space to turn toward welcoming the Word, to incline the ear of our hearts, so to speak.

From this stillness, we can begin to "Listen." Listening is a fundamental step toward an open spiritual disposition, a receptivity to the living Word of God who is ever faithful in addressing us. This spiritual skill alone, if we hone it, can already make an enormous difference in our communication with others, whether face-to-face, through a screen, or anything in between. We cannot communicate well if we do not know how to pause and listen, offering hospitality to the word (of God and of others) through this simple and profound act of communication. Listening welcomes the Word and allows it to address us. A word or phrase that catches our attention as we listen becomes an invitation to enter into a sacred space, to begin to discover the meaning the Divine Word holds for our lives this day.

The "Reflect" section then offers food for thought about the theme of communication in each scriptural selection. But these reflections should not limit you as you enter more deeply into conversation with the Word. Much more may come to mind in your own reflection and prayer.

The questions offered in the "Ponder" sections are likewise meant as guides, especially for those who journal, helping to deepen contemplation not just of the Scripture text but especially of how the text speaks to your life and where there might be opportunities for growth or conversion.

Finally, the "Pray" section helps us lift the fruit of our prayerful reflection back up to God. Of course, you are welcome to use the prayers provided or pray in your own words in response to Scripture and your reflection on it.

Benedictine sister Joan Chittister reminds us that the way we communicate will determine the quality of our lives as well as the lives of those we touch.[6] The way my children have appropriated and now *reflect back* Christian worship in their own unique ways brings me joy and wonder. It is precisely through their communication of faith that I am touched by that joy. I am not sure how else I would be aware of it, this intimate response to God's Spirit that is stirring their little souls. They communicate it, and it is gift and joy.

[6] Joan Chittister, "The 11th Step: What We Say, and How We Say It, Defines Us," *National Catholic Reporter* 56, no. 8 (January 24, 2020): 17.

Communicating faith is ultimately about *living it and sharing it with others*, in word, deed, and witness of life. It is at the deepest core of who we are as Christians, and at the deepest core of who the church is. Whether we are sharing faith in the family, posting it on social media, publishing it in an article, or preaching it from a pulpit, authentic communication of the faith is integral to our identity as Christians. When moved by the Spirit, it is gift and joy.

May God's Spirit come and give us the ability to speak, as the Spirit did in that Upper Room on Pentecost Day. May our words too reach out and truly communicate Good News, build up people and communities, and inspire others with hope, possibility, and new life.

Daniella Zsupan-Jerome
Collegeville, MN

1

God Said

(Genesis 1:1-5)

STATIO: Become still in body and mind. Take a minute to breathe and be aware of the moment.

LISTEN: What word or phrase stands out to you?

In the beginning, when God created the heavens and the earth—and the earth was without form or shape, with darkness over the abyss and a mighty wind sweeping over the waters—

Then God said: Let there be light, and there was light. God saw that the light was good. God then separated the light from the darkness. God called the light "day," and the darkness he called "night." Evening came, and morning followed—the first day.

The Word of the Lord.

REFLECT: *God said.* In the very first words of the Bible, we encounter God communicating. We are nothing. We do not yet exist. The earth is without form. There is only darkness. God is the only one who is. The Spirit is a mighty wind sweeping over the waters, and God is about to speak and express divine reason. God says, "Let there be," and there is. This dynamic of Word and Spirit uttering creation reveals God in the beginning of time.

God's Word brings all of reality into being. God's Word is creative. It is life-giving. It is reality itself which pours out into creation to bring it into existence. Creation is born of God's communication, from light and darkness, to the sky and the earth, to the water and the dry land, to the plants and the seasons, to the stars and the living creatures, to man and woman. All exists because God's Word and Spirit *say it* to be so. The power of God's Word and Spirit to bring forth life is our first profound lesson for faithful communication.

I have worked in the world of academia for over a decade. During this time it has been remarkable to note how communication unfolds in the classroom, in the conference hall, in the faculty meeting, and these days, in academic circles on social media. Very often, and not without good reason, this is a culture that values the question, the challenge, the debate, the contrary opinion, and the contest of wits and intellect. This approach has its merits: it encourages thought and reflection and can lead to new insights and new learning. At the same time, for faithful communication, it also carries a risk: communication becoming contest, and connection becoming conquering another with our words. In such an approach there are winners and losers. And we lose sight of the true potential of communication for building communion and bringing forth new life.

The same dynamic is often present in digital culture. Comment feeds are often battlefields for the last word, the clever quip, the mic-drop phrase. Engaging in a debate becomes a public performance and draws an audience there for the drama, heightened by algorithms that serve to foster content engagement above all. To this point, there are numerous memes about comment feed culture that show a popcorn-eating audience viewing the drama. In the midst of this dynamic, it is difficult to remain committed to life-giving language, and indeed, regard for conversation partners as persons of dignity and inherent value. The commitment to this mindset is a discipline, and a spiritual disposition for our time.

Dedicating our communication practices to giving life can be as simple as a daily prayer. As a person who researches social communication, it has always touched me that in the liturgical tradition of daily prayer, each morning begins with the short invocation from Psalm 51: "Lord, open my lips. And my mouth will proclaim your praise." The universal church begins each new day with a prayer about good communication! With this, the beginning of each new day also recalls creation, God's "Let there be" that brings light out of darkness, order out of chaos, life out of nothing. Beginning the new day by asking God to open our lips for praise is a powerful prayer about faithful communication, aligning our words with God's life-giving ones. Through it, the believer seeks to stand in the Spirit, the same Spirit who at creation carried God's life-giving Words of "Let there be."

God said, "Let there be," and there was. The Divine Word brings forth life and creates a context in which life can continue to grow and flourish. Our conversations too can bring forth life, whether in the form of new insights, new perspectives, or new ideas. After all, the exercise of our intellectual creativity, properly ordered, gives honor to the Creator whose life and breath we carry. But when intellectual creativity becomes intellectual conquest, we must discern whether what we are doing is life-giving. If it humiliates and tears a person down, if we shine at the expense of others, we are sapping life instead of nurturing it. Rather, our words can give form and shape to new ideas, ours and others', as we strive to honor the Creator with our conversations.

PONDER: God's Word gives life. How do my words reflect this? What does creation teach us about communication?

PRAY: Creator God, you breathed "Let there be," and it was. Your Word and Spirit brought everything into being as you communicated your love for us and called us into love through the act of creation. Send that same Word and Spirit now so we can learn to communicate with love like you do. Bless our prayer and reflection so our words too might give life. We ask this through your Son, the Word Incarnate, by the power of your Spirit, the breath of life. Amen.

2

Adam Speaks

(Genesis 2:4-7, 18-23)

STATIO: Become still in body and mind. Take a minute to breathe and be aware of the moment.

LISTEN: What word or phrase stands out to you?

This is the story of the heavens and the earth at their creation. When the LORD God made the earth and the heavens—there was no field shrub on earth and no grass of the field had sprouted, for the LORD God had sent no rain upon the earth and there was no man to till the ground, but a stream was welling up out of the earth and watering all the surface of the ground—then the LORD God formed the man out of the dust of the ground and blew into his nostrils the breath of life, and the man became a living being. . . .

The LORD God said: It is not good for the man to be alone. I will make a helper suited to him. So the LORD God formed out of the ground all the wild animals and all the birds of the air, and he brought them to the man to see what he would call them; whatever the man called each living creature was then its name. The man gave names to all the tame animals, all the birds of the air, and all the wild animals; but none proved to be a helper suited to the man.

So the Lord *God cast a deep sleep on the man, and while he was asleep, he took out one of his ribs and closed up its place with flesh. The* Lord *God then built the rib that he had taken from the man into a woman. When he brought her to the man, the man said:*

"This one, at last, is bone of my bones
and flesh of my flesh;
This one shall be called 'woman,'
for out of man this one has been taken."

The Word of the Lord.

REFLECT: After God's Word and Spirit pour out into creation, God fashions the human person out of clay. God breathes the Spirit into the clay, giving Adam life. Adam becomes a living being in the image and likeness of God. Now he also carries within him that same life-giving Spirit that hovered above the dark waters, the same life-giving Spirit that accompanied God's Word when God said, "Let there be."

Like God, Adam can also speak. His first words of naming the animals point to God. Naming the animals shows his creativity, his blessed identity as one made in the Creator's image. There is something beautiful about God leading the animals to Adam so he can discover his gift. Through Adam's first words, God the loving Father, God the Teacher, begins to show the human person who he is, a living being in the image and likeness of God.

Scripture does not record these first words. The first words that are recorded are about Adam meeting his equal, Eve, from the bone of his bones, and the flesh of his flesh. In their encounter, we hear the words of a joyful Adam, one whose mouth is full of praise. At last! She fills a yearning in him that he did not even know he had. In her, he recognizes mutuality, communion, being one body with this other, who is both different but also the same. Adam's first words in Scripture speak of communion. He praises the communion that humankind is called to live, the beautiful self-gift, given in mutuality that is shared between man and woman. And he praises this joyfully because this communion too is in the image and likeness of God. Adam, who carries the breath of God, offers his first words honoring the Creator and honoring the divine communion that God is and that God calls us into.

Social media calls us into a cacophony of communication. As I scroll down the screen, one thing follows another: a cooking video, a funny meme, a person looking for recommendations on a new appliance, a picture of a friend's new haircut, the latest article about the pope or the president, and so on, and so on. But once in a while in this endless scroll, there is a gathering point, a true sense of connection that gives us pause. A friend suffering from cancer receives an outpouring of prayers and comments. A photo of a newborn receives hundreds of congrats. Even if it is just for a moment, we glimpse communion and feel that joy, that compassion, that community. At last!

It used to be proper social practice to share significant news in person. Now, the norm is making one's good news public on social media. As I recall recent examples of hearing joyful or important news, it strikes me that the majority came to me through social media. I recently shared via social media my own news of a professional achievement. The response from others brought me lots of joy and a brief glimpse of communion through all the good people who signaled their presence to me that day. In the midst of the ordinary, endless scrolling experience, this was an "At last" day. As people of faith, we should pay attention to these "At last" moments on social media and ponder how we may lend our presence to bringing these about.

We are made for God and for one another. In the cacophony of social media, our connections are mostly casual, as passers-by on a busy digital road. Whenever we do have a joyful moment of encounter, it gives us pause. It stops us in our scrolling, and we sense something bigger than ourselves. Christian spirituality holds that this joy we find in one another, the joy of encounter and community, is something holy. It is a holy joy because it draws us out of ourselves, and, ultimately, toward God. Our communication is both an expression of this movement toward holiness and a way to deepen it. May our words echo those of Adam whenever we encounter one another. At last.

PONDER: What brings me joy about communication? Have I had "At last" moments in the digital context?

PRAY: Creator of Heaven and Earth, you breathed life into Adam, and he spoke in your image, uttering words of creativity, joy, communion, and praise. Breathe your Spirit into our clay hearts so we too can offer words that are life-giving, joyful, and revelatory of your Word and Spirit. Bless our words so they can bring about communion. We ask this through your Son, the Word Incarnate, by the power of the Spirit. Amen.

3

Twisting Words

(Genesis 3:1-13)

STATIO: Become still in body and mind. Take a minute to breathe and be aware of the moment.

LISTEN: What word or phrase stands out to you?

Now the snake was the most cunning of all the wild animals that the LORD God had made. He asked the woman, "Did God really say, 'You shall not eat from any of the trees in the garden'?" The woman answered the snake: "We may eat of the fruit of the trees in the garden; it is only about the fruit of the tree in the middle of the garden that God said, 'You shall not eat it or even touch it, or else you will die.'" But the snake said to the woman: "You certainly will not die! God knows well that when you eat of it your eyes will be opened and you will be like gods, who know good and evil." The woman saw that the tree was good for food and pleasing to the eyes, and the tree was desirable for gaining wisdom. So she took some of its fruit and ate it; and she also gave some to her husband, who was with her, and he ate it. Then the eyes of both of them were opened, and they knew that they were naked; so they sewed fig leaves together and made loin-cloths for themselves.

When they heard the sound of the Lord *God walking about in the garden at the breezy time of the day, the man and his wife hid themselves from the* Lord *God among the trees of the garden. The* Lord *God then called to the man and asked him: Where are you? He answered, "I heard you in the garden; but I was afraid, because I was naked, so I hid." Then God asked: Who told you that you were naked? Have you eaten from the tree of which I had forbidden you to eat? The man replied, "The woman whom you put here with me—she gave me fruit from the tree, so I ate it." The* Lord *God then asked the woman: What is this you have done? The woman answered, "The snake tricked me, so I ate it."*

The Word of the Lord.

REFLECT: God's life-giving Word echoes through creation. Adam's first words are full of creativity, joy, and communion. It is all the more tragic, then, that the fall of humankind also comes about from a communicative act: a deceptive conversation. The snake's conversation with Eve is one that seeks to plant seeds of mistrust and doubt, suspicion and separation from God. The snake is cunning and deceitful. It could not care less about the fruit of the tree in question. What the snake wants is our separation from God. It therefore twists the truth and suggests that God is not who we think God is. Hearing a few choice words from the Father of Lies ("Did God really say . . . ?"), man and woman begin to wonder, *Did God really give us creation, give us life, give us Godself in love?* Because, in fact, that is what God does when God *says.*

Did God really say? Man and woman begin to falter in their trust in God. They think that God hasn't given Godself to them already in communion, that God has some ulterior motive. They begin to think that God's Words mean something other than life and gift and communion. This is news to Adam and Eve, since in the garden all they have known is God's blessings and providence. They have come to know God walking in the cool of the evening together as Loving Creator and Parent. What is God holding back? They begin to suspect and separate—and with that, the snake wins.

Did God really say? And so, with a few twisted words, man and woman fall out of communion with God. They listen to a voice other than God's. A voice whose words take life away and offer instead falsehood, meaninglessness, and despair.

Reflecting on the twisted words of the snake, we can see the harm that intentional falsehood and deception bring. The fallout is spiritual and interpersonal. When we do not communicate truthfully, the result is a detrimental loss of trust. And the loss of trust is deeply destabilizing. Recent still in our memory, the 2020 COVID pandemic turned our world upside down with fear, confusion, and twisted words. In addition to the health crisis itself, one of the daily struggles during this time was communication: not always knowing what information was truthful and reliable. Quarantined and huddled around our screens for more information about the disease, our anxiety grew as fake news, conspiracy theories, angry comments, and fearmongering began to appear alongside the facts. The snake was coiling once again, aiming at our stability of heart, our trust in God and one another. Like original sin, we are still living with the impact.

I have a good friend who is quite provocative on social media. They enjoy posting edgy political commentary, often with sarcastic humor. They also enjoy taking part in the animated discussion this type of content invites. If I did not know my friend in person, their edgy online presence would be intimidating and even off-putting for me. I am not sure I would hang around. But, because I know and like my friend (who happens to be a good and kind person), I am able to receive their edgy content with a measure of acceptance and trust. Knowing and trusting one another makes all the difference when it comes to good and faithful communication.

To live well in community and to abide in the joy of communion, we need basic trust. Truthful communication is an essential building block of this trust. Deceptive words are not only a moral problem, they are also a spiritual one. When trust in the truth of communication gives way to confusion and despair, we once again find ourselves falling, separating from God and one another. May we find footing with the Word of God whenever such words unsettle, upset, or frighten.

PONDER: The snake's words are subtle. What are the subtle voices trying to divert my attention away from God? How can I resist these voices?

PRAY: Merciful God, you made us garments even when we hid from you in shame (Gen 3:21). You remain faithful even when we are unfaithful. Spare us from the twisted path of the enemy.

Allow your life-giving Word to make straight the way of the truth. Teach us to stay committed to the truth, and with the truth to turn with mind and heart back into communion with you through your Son, who is the way, the truth, and the life (John 14:6). May your Spirit of truth guide us always (John 16:13). Amen.

4

Tower of Babel

(Genesis 11:1-9)

STATIO: Become still in body and mind. Take a minute to breathe and be aware of the moment.

LISTEN: What word or phrase stands out to you?

The whole world had the same language and the same words. When they were migrating from the east, they came to a valley in the land of Shinar and settled there. They said to one another, "Come, let us mold bricks and harden them with fire." They used bricks for stone, and bitumen for mortar. Then they said, "Come, let us build ourselves a city and a tower with its top in the sky, and so make a name for ourselves; otherwise we shall be scattered all over the earth."

The Lord *came down to see the city and the tower that the people had built. Then the* Lord *said: If now, while they are one people and all have the same language, they have started to do this, nothing they presume to do will be out of their reach. Come, let us go down and there confuse their language, so that no one will understand the speech of another. So the* Lord *scattered them from there over all the earth, and they stopped building the city. That is why it was called Babel, because there the LORD confused the speech of all the world. From there the LORD scattered them over all the earth.*

The Word of the Lord.

REFLECT: A pattern begins to form after the fall as humankind grows in relationship with God: sin, grace, and sin again. After the fall, fratricide (Gen 4:1-16), and the flood (Gen 7), God makes a covenant with all humankind (and every living creature), promising never to flood the earth again (Gen 9:1-17). This is a fresh start, a restoration of harmony between God and human beings. And the first story in response to this grace is of prideful human beings taking matters into their own hands *again*.

This time we try to make a name for ourselves by building a tower that reaches the heavens. To do this, we turn to communication. We use our same language and our same words to try to dethrone God, to collude against God's will and order. We use our same language to raise ourselves up to heaven by our own efforts. Not so different from Adam and Eve taking the fruit of the tree into their own hands.

Using communication, God's very gift toward communion, to conspire against God is a deep sacrilege. It is a desecration of language itself, uprooting it from the foundation in communion that would bind us to God and to one another. This is not true communication. There is no gift of self, offered in love. Rather it is a separation from and a challenge to God, as we shout our pride at heaven with every brick and stone. In building the tower, we forget what language is for; we forget its aim in communication toward communion. We abuse the sanctity of language, uproot it from its foundation in the Divine Word and the Breath of Life. And so God takes it away from us.

When God confuses the languages, God is simply holding up a mirror. In conspiring to dethrone God by our own efforts, we are in fact creating separation. We are sowing seeds of division. We are spreading out further from one another and from God. And so, God grants the consequences of our actions. We can no longer understand each other and will have to learn—through much effort, humility, and discipline—how to be a human family. Like Adam and Eve, we will now toil and labor even to communicate, awaiting the grace of Word and Spirit to show us another way.

My family immigrated to the United States over thirty years ago from Budapest, Hungary. As a child facing that transition, one of my biggest fears was not knowing the English language. Immersed as a foreign child into an American middle school, it took a lot of work, humility, and courage to eventually feel a sense of belonging, community, and communion. Immigrants know deeply the isolation and humility caused by a language barrier. We also feel deeply the gestures of hospitality extended by those who are willing to break through that barrier.

Today, in my classroom, I regularly have students for whom English is a second (or third or fourth!) language. I am deeply sympathetic to the familiar process of humility, courage, and hard work I see in them. I also have learned that the avenues of communication are varied. One can be an excellent writer but struggle with pronunciation. Similarly, some may be exuberant in spirit and rich in presence, while others may be withdrawn and take longer to get to know. Communication and the sharing of one's presence can happen in many ways. When it comes to faithful communication, looking for these multiple ways is a gesture of hospitality we are all called to when forging connections and building community with one another. Meeting people where they are and inviting them to share who they are in their own ways is an act of humility on our part, as we step into this humble space with them. It honors the very way Christ humbled himself to be one with us.

Humility can be tough but also very good for the spirit, especially when we are tempted to raise towers. In humility we stay close to the ground, close to the earth out of which God fashioned us. In humility we come to know our need, our dependence on God and others, more deeply. This knowledge then becomes wisdom that lifts us out of ourselves to God and community.

In humility we learn that we are never independent agents, lone rangers following our own personal missions or desires. We are created in relationship with God and for relationship with God and others. We are made for communion, and our communication is a sacred gift.

PONDER: How has pride hurt my communication with others? How is bad communication an obstacle to communion?

PRAY: Just and Merciful God, you invite us into covenant time and time again, ever faithful to your promise of communion. Send your Spirit to guide us away from selfish pride and the misuse of language that would separate us from you and from others. Allow our words to be words of covenant and communion, building not towers but community, not a name for ourselves but always honoring your divine name. We ask this in the most holy name of Jesus Christ, by the power of the Spirit. Amen.

5

The Lord Spoke to Her

(Genesis 16:1-16)

STATIO: Become still in body and mind. Take a minute to breathe and be aware of the moment.

LISTEN: What word or phrase stands out to you?

Abram's wife Sarai had borne him no children. Now she had an Egyptian maidservant named Hagar. Sarai said to Abram: "The LORD has kept me from bearing children. Have intercourse with my maid; perhaps I will have sons through her." Abram obeyed Sarai. Thus, after Abram had lived ten years in the land of Canaan, his wife Sarai took her maid, Hagar the Egyptian, and gave her to her husband Abram to be his wife. He had intercourse with her, and she became pregnant. As soon as Hagar knew she was pregnant, her mistress lost stature in her eyes. So Sarai said to Abram: "This outrage against me is your fault. I myself gave my maid to your embrace; but ever since she knew she was pregnant, I have lost stature in her eyes. May the LORD decide between you and me!" Abram told Sarai: "Your maid is in your power.

Do to her what you regard as right." Sarai then mistreated her so much that Hagar ran away from her.

The LORD's angel found her by a spring in the wilderness, the spring on the road to Shur, and he asked, "Hagar, maid of Sarai, where have you come from and where are you going?" She answered, "I am running away from my mistress, Sarai." But the LORD's angel told her: "Go back to your mistress and submit to her authority. I will make your descendants so numerous," added the LORD's angel, "that they will be too many to count." Then the LORD's angel said to her:

"You are now pregnant and shall bear a son;
you shall name him Ishmael,
For the LORD has heeded your affliction.
He shall be a wild ass of a man,
his hand against everyone,
and everyone's hand against him;
Alongside all his kindred
shall he encamp."

To the LORD who spoke to her she gave a name, saying, "You are God who sees me"; she meant, "Have I really seen God and remained alive after he saw me?" That is why the well is called Beer-lahai-roi. It is between Kadesh and Bered.

Hagar bore Abram a son, and Abram named the son whom Hagar bore him Ishmael. Abram was eighty-six years old when Hagar bore him Ishmael.

The Word of the Lord.

REFLECT: Angels are messengers of God, witnesses and bearers of the Word to humankind. The angel's visit to Hagar is the first of such visits in Scripture. Angels will come time and time again, most remarkably perhaps to a young woman in a town of Galilee called Nazareth, centuries later. But it is also remarkable that the first angelic word in Scripture comes to Hagar, a servant woman, a stranger and foreigner, forced into sex and pregnancy, who then is mistreated and cast out in anger simply for doing what she was supposed to do. Now she is alone, wandering the desert in her pain and desperation, a person with no power whatsoever and yet the weight of the world upon her. God's Word finds this person in this first angelic visit.

In the stories of Scripture, angels do not chit chat. They do not sugarcoat. They bring truth, assurance, clarity, and direction. They bring the divine, life-giving Word and let it resound in all its power. Hagar is encouraged to return and to allow God to bring abundance and life out of her predicament. These words are promise and strength to a woman used and cast aside. They are the Words of a God Who Sees Her. Unlike those building the tower of Babel who wished to make a name for themselves, because of her encounter with God, Hagar recognizes and honors God's name, and she does so in a deeply personal way.

God's Word often comes to prophets and patriarchs, leaders of the people. But it also comes in a profound way to the lowest of the low. In this way, we are once again called back to the value of humility. Flowing out of another angelic visit, Mary's words will remind us that God casts the mighty from their thrones but lifts up the lowly (Luke 1:52). When we are keenly aware of our own limitations and finitude, we are perhaps better disposed to the Divine Word than when we fancy ourselves to be on top of the world. In this same vein we are also called to seek and honor the voices of those speaking from lowliness, from the margins.

In the influencer-driven context of digital culture, "likes," "subscribes," and "follows" matter. People are deemed significant if their content generates a lot of interaction from others. Yet I wonder if this a good metric for human dignity and values. I am moved by the example of a friend who has overcome a lot of mental health challenges. They now make it a daily habit to post authentic, uplifting content from their life on social media. Knowing my friend's story, I perceive this to be a part of their healing and self-care, a commitment to themselves to seek and appreciate life. Their daily postings generate very little visible interaction. Still, they just keep at it. I have come to anticipate their updates and believe that these genuine moments of human sharing matter more than the popular or viral content in my social media feed.

In digital culture, we are immersed in information. One of the ongoing challenges of our cultural context is how to rank and sort the many voices present in this constant flow. Algorithms prioritize for us the words and voices we encounter, and the ranking of these is often economic, political, or based on the most profitable outcome for the social media platforms we use. Who are the lowly whose voices need to be lifted up in this context? More profoundly, who are the ones unseen, lost in the vast landscape of digital culture, yearning to meet the God Who Sees Them? How might we be like the messenger to Hagar, dignifying and encouraging the lowly with our words today?

PONDER: How does justice feature into faithful communication? Should there be a preferential option for the lowly when we discern how to share God's Word? Who are the lowly when it comes to social communication today?

PRAY: God of Compassion and Justice, your Word comes to prophets and patriarchs throughout Scripture, but it also comes to lift up the lowly, speaking powerfully to those who need to hear it most. Send your Spirit to embolden us to speak Good News to the lowly and to see the face of your Son in their midst. Give us words of promise, encouragement, and hope as we accompany those on the margins. We ask this through your Son, by the power of the Spirit. Amen.

6

His Dreams and His Reports

(Genesis 37:1-11)

STATIO: Become still in body and mind. Take a minute to breathe and be aware of the moment.

LISTEN: What word or phrase stands out to you?

Jacob settled in the land where his father had sojourned, the land of Canaan. This is the story of the family of Jacob. When Joseph was seventeen years old, he was tending the flocks with his brothers; he was an assistant to the sons of his father's wives Bilhah and Zilpah, and Joseph brought their father bad reports about them. Israel loved Joseph best of all his sons, for he was the child of his old age; and he had made him a long ornamented tunic. When his brothers saw that their father loved him best of all his brothers, they hated him so much that they could not say a kind word to him.

Once Joseph had a dream, and when he told his brothers, they hated him even more. He said to them, "Listen to this dream I had. There were we, binding sheaves in the field, when suddenly my sheaf rose to an upright position, and your sheaves formed a ring around my sheaf and bowed down to it." His brothers said to him, "Are you really going to make yourself king over us? Will you rule over us?" So they hated him all the more because of his dreams and his reports.

Then he had another dream, and told it to his brothers. "Look, I had another dream," he said; "this time, the sun and the moon and eleven stars were bowing down to me." When he told it to his father and his brothers, his father reproved him and asked, "What is the meaning of this dream of yours? Can it be that I and your mother and your brothers are to come and bow to the ground before you?" So his brothers were furious at him but his father kept the matter in mind.

The Word of the Lord.

REFLECT: Joseph, son of Jacob, is not the first to encounter the presence of God through dreams. Receiving divine inspiration through dreams ran in the family. We see this unique ability in Jacob, who in his dreams saw angels descending from and ascending to the heavens (Gen 28:12). Jacob also found divine inspiration in his dreams about how to profit from Laban's flock (Gen 31:10). But while Jacob's dreams brought him blessings and inspiration, Joseph's dreams, at first, nearly cost him his life. As the story goes, Joseph's brothers' hatred turns to action: first they cast him into a pit, then they sell him into slavery.

Joseph's ability to interpret dreams is a unique gift of communication. In the ancient world, dreams were considered revelatory, prophetic even, and were regarded as a means of supernatural insight. To interpret dreams was therefore a gift of prophecy, a gift of revealing the mystery of the Divine Word.

But Joseph's family is not able to hold or nurture this budding and extraordinary gift. The relationship between the brothers is broken. If communication is the indicator of a healthy relationship, here we meet brothers who cannot even muster a kind word to one of their own. Joseph's words of mystery are met with hatred; his vision of truth is met with a threat to his life.

There is a hard lesson here for all of us about what it means to be a speaker of God's Word, no matter what. When God's Word comes to us, whether through a dream, a prayer, or another means of inspiration, it embraces us totally. It sets our hearts burning. We *must* speak about it (Jer 20:9). So also with Joseph, who was not at all on good terms with his brothers and who might have fared better keeping his mouth shut. Instead of retreating further from his brothers, he insists on communicating with them. He risks it all and *commands* them: *Listen to this dream that I dreamed!* Then he shares his strange, prophetic dream, not once but *twice*, even though there is already fury and hatred in his brothers' hearts. Is he the first martyr for God's Word, compelled to speak the truth, come what may? He almost is, though he is spared and vindicated by the end of the story when the brothers—starving and seeking alms from Egypt—bow down before him, just as he had dreamed (Gen 42:6).

When God's Word comes to us, we are taken up into it. We become bearers of the Word, serving the truth with boldness, courage, and enthusiasm. Some will be inspired in turn by our sharing of this Word. Some will want to silence us, throw us in a pit, sell us into slavery, or stretch us out on a tree. Spreading the Word of God is not for the faint of heart. But there is no worthier task, no better news, no fuller life.

I do not engage on comment feeds often. I am more of an observer of the conversations that take place there. Of the few times I have entered into an exchange, one instance stands out. One day I shared a positive news story about some new initiative taken up by the church's hierarchy. Several people liked or affirmed the piece, but one person replied with strong and deeply felt sentiments about the marginalization of same-sex couples by the Catholic Church. As the piece did not treat this topic, this comment was coming from a personal place, reflective of this person's journey and experience. My comment feed was going to be the place where this journey found expression for him that day. I sat and stared at my screen for a good while, discerning how to respond. I paced my room, came back, rehearsed options in my head. As a Roman Catholic theologian and a person who publicly thinks about social communication and faith, I was feeling some pressure. I wanted to respond with mercy and truth and with integrity. I wanted to respond like Christ. I also wanted to welcome Christ in the stranger having come to my comment feed that day. After some time, it finally came to me. "Peace be with you," I posted.

I still do not comment much these days, but I have gained appreciation for what it means to seek prudence and wrestle with how to respond in faith to a conflicted comment. In our digital context, conflict is plentiful: conversation threads often blow up rather quickly with vitriolic speech. It is not at all easy to remain steady and be present in difficult conversations. When feeling pressure, we can come and go very easily in these digital spaces, walking away from conflict and, more importantly, from the interpersonal consequences of conflict. We can "cancel," mute, or "unfriend" one another and call it a day.

There is a prophetic call in staying put and working through interpersonal conflict in these otherwise fluid spaces where the social bonds are much looser than those with our friends and family. In digital culture, we can just fight and walk away. But what are we losing in the process, when we miss the profound and difficult process of working through a conflict?

PONDER: How have I met resistance in my efforts to share God's Word?

PRAY: Loving God, your Word comes to us in many mysterious ways: prayers, dreams, moments of inspiration, moments of unexpected grace. Your Word also comes to us most fully in your Son, Jesus Christ, the Perfect Communicator, who was crucified and is risen for the life of the world. Prepare our hearts with the consolation and courage of the Spirit to be fearless bearers of your Word, and to trust in your Spirit when the words we give are met with hostility or hatefulness. Give us faith so that with our words we may enter boldly into the death of Christ so as to rise with him to new life. Grant this through Christ our Lord, by the power of the Spirit. Amen.

7

Take to Heart These Words

(Deuteronomy 6:1-9)

STATIO: Become still in body and mind. Take a minute to breathe and be aware of the moment.

LISTEN: What word or phrase stands out to you?

This then is the commandment, the statutes and the ordinances, which the LORD, your God, has commanded that you be taught to observe in the land you are about to cross into to possess, so that you, that is, you, your child, and your grandchild, may fear the LORD, your God, by keeping, as long as you live, all his statutes and commandments which I enjoin on you, and thus have long life. Hear then, Israel, and be careful to observe them, that it may go well with you and that you may increase greatly; for the LORD, the God of your ancestors, promised you a land flowing with milk and honey.

Hear, O Israel! The LORD is our God, the LORD alone! Therefore, you shall love the LORD, your God, with your whole heart, and with your whole being, and with your whole strength. Take to heart these words which I command you today. Keep repeating them to your children. Recite them when you are at home and when you are away, when you lie down and when you get up. Bind them on your arm as a sign and let them be as a pendant on your forehead. Write them on the doorposts of your houses and on your gates.

The Word of the Lord.

REFLECT: We hear in this passage the beginning of the ancient Jewish prayer, the Shema Yisrael (Hear, Israel), which still forms the centerpiece of Jewish devotional life today. Devout Jews recite this prayer multiple times daily.

It is profound and beautiful that this prayer comes in Scripture right after Moses recalls the covenant at Horeb and reminds the people of the Ten Commandments (Deut 5). After those extraordinary revelatory experiences of God, it all comes down to one basic message, one unsurpassable string of words: *The LORD is our God, the LORD alone! Therefore, you shall love the LORD, your God, with your whole heart, and with your whole being, and with your whole strength.*

In a tradition that holds 613 *mitzvot* or commandments, repeating these ultimate words each day about who God is and who his people are called to be offers a sound framework for understanding religious practice. All the law and commandments are about these essential words.

Along these lines, Moses exhorts the people to "take to heart these words" about their love for the One God. Their constant reflection on the covenant and the law is meant to take form in the daily recitation of these words, focusing on them as the life-giving center of their whole tradition. So important is the love of the One God that the people are meant to be immersed in these words: they are to recite them, tell them to their children, wear them, and inscribe them on the doorposts of their homes. They are to take every measure not to forget the profound truth of these words, with the hope that full immersion into these words will be so transformative that the words will take root in people's hearts.

As Christians we too are part of the same covenant, and part of the same call to love the One God and take to heart these words. Some of our saints are people whose immersion into God's Words shined off of them. The way they expressed themselves, the way they communicated, was full of the Word. One such example was St. Benedict of Nursia, monastic and author of the famous Rule of St. Benedict. The Rule of Benedict is a relatively short text about living life in community and being centered on Christ. At the same time, it includes over 320 biblical references, at times woven in quite seamlessly. In the Rule we see the scriptural Word as integral to Benedict's own language. He writes as one immersed in the Word.

Reminiscent of the Shema, Benedict begins his Rule with the invitation to listen with the ear of our hearts. The heart is the core, the center of who we are. What we allow in the heart will shape our communication and our way of being in the world. Wise in faith, Moses and Benedict both urge us to fill our hearts, then, with God's Word.

In our digital culture, we have a steady stream of words (and sounds and images) seeking our attention. The social media scroll can be endless, bringing before us posting after posting. Ought we absorb it all? What we see and hear also shapes the way we express ourselves. We have taken terms like

#hashtag, abbreviations like "LOL," and language forms like the meme, the GIF, and the emoji into everyday self-expression. Digitality is taking root in our hearts.

For faithful communication, there is an important invitation here about discernment. What are the uplifting and life-giving aspects of digital culture, and where should we be more guarded about our hearts, our time, our attention spans? At the end of a long day, I have often picked up my phone and scrolled on social media for a while to de-stress. I intend to scroll for a short while and sometimes catch myself thirty minutes later, still doing the same thing. I wonder about habits like this and how they are filling my mind and heart. Even more so, how is scrolling filling me in such a way that I am able to give of myself to others the next day? Opening the heart is always coupled with the invitation to give of ourselves to others in love, especially when it comes to faithful communication.

Our hearts ultimately desire God's Word. Christ revealed the Divine Word to us not on tablets of stone but by the presence, witness, death, and resurrection of his very self. To immerse ourselves in the Word is encounter and relationship with Christ. From this spiritual ground, we are called to be communicators of the Word in turn. Toward this, we ponder: How are we aware of God's Word? In what ways are we immersed in the Word? In what ways do we take it to heart? And how might all of this give form to our communication?

PONDER: How do I remind myself of the importance of God's Word? What devotions, practices, or symbols help me immerse myself in the Word?

PRAY: God of the Covenant, you revealed your Words to your prophets who called your people to be faithful to them and take them to heart. In Jesus Christ we have the fullness of your Word. Teach us to take his Good News to heart, and to immerse ourselves in the Divine Word the way your people once did in the desert while traveling to the Promised Land. As we walk our own paths of faith, send your Holy Spirit alongside us, to remind us and guide us into the truth of your Words. We ask this in the name of Jesus Christ, by the power of the Spirit. Amen.

8

Listening Together

(1 Samuel 3:1-18)

STATIO: Become still in body and mind. Take a minute to breathe and be aware of the moment.

LISTEN: What word or phrase stands out to you?

During the time young Samuel was minister to the LORD under Eli, the word of the LORD was scarce and vision infrequent. One day Eli was asleep in his usual place. His eyes had lately grown so weak that he could not see. The lamp of God was not yet extinguished, and Samuel was sleeping in the temple of the LORD where the ark of God was. The LORD called to Samuel, who answered, "Here I am." He ran to Eli and said, "Here I am. You called me." "I did not call you," Eli answered. "Go back to sleep." So he went back to sleep. Again the LORD called Samuel, who rose and went to Eli. "Here I am," he said. "You called me." But he answered, "I did not call you, my son. Go back to sleep."

Samuel did not yet recognize the LORD, since the word of the LORD had not yet been revealed to him. The LORD called Samuel again, for the third time. Getting up and going to Eli, he said, "Here I am. You called me." Then Eli understood that the LORD was calling the youth. So he said to Samuel, "Go to sleep, and if you are called, reply, 'Speak, LORD, for your servant is listening.'" When Samuel went to sleep in his place, the LORD came and stood there, calling out as before: Samuel, Samuel! Samuel answered, "Speak, for your servant is listening." The LORD said to Samuel: I am about to do something in Israel that will make the ears of everyone who hears it ring. On that day I will carry out against Eli everything I have said about his house, beginning to end. I announce to him that I am condemning his house once and for all, because of this crime: though he knew his sons were blaspheming God, he did not reprove them. Therefore, I swear to Eli's house: No sacrifice or offering will ever expiate its crime. Samuel then slept until morning, when he got up early and opened the doors of the temple of the LORD. He was afraid to tell Eli the vision, but Eli called to him, "Samuel, my son!" He replied, "Here I am." Then Eli asked, "What did he say to you? Hide nothing from me! May God do thus to you, and more, if you hide from me a single thing he told you." So Samuel told him everything, and held nothing back. Eli answered, "It is the LORD. What is pleasing in the LORD's sight, the LORD will do."

The Word of the Lord.

REFLECT: At a time when the Word of the Lord is scarce and visions infrequent, a little boy sleeps in the temple to beckon the Word. Sleeping in sanctuaries was an ancient practice to invite visions and inspire dreams, and so Samuel's bed is made near the ark in hopes of such a vision. God does not disappoint.

What is beautiful about the way God's Word comes is that it invites conversation and community around it. The boy receives the Word, but does not understand what is happening, nor does he know how to respond. He runs three times to Eli, the high priest and elder in charge of raising Samuel in the faith and service of the Lord. Eli is a wise man; he does not even blink at the fact that the Word addresses Samuel directly. Instead he humbly guides the boy to respond to the Word of God. "Speak, LORD, for your servant is listening," becomes one of the wisest human statements in the Bible.

Seemingly, the message of God's Word has little to do with Samuel and much to do with Eli and God's wrath against his household, thanks to his rebellious sons Hophni and Phinehas. Yet the Divine Word and Divine Wisdom are revealed together as a boy and a high priest must listen together to experience God's communication. The boy has ears to hear God's call. But the older man has wisdom, training, and a sense of the tradition to be able to understand the Word and live by its message. Samuel learns from Eli how to discern the Divine Word and respond to it humbly. And Eli learns that our Almighty God is not too great to address the smallest in our midst. Perhaps this is where it started for the boy who would become the great prophet Samuel: an experience of the Word, a personal call, a strong divine message calling for justice. And Eli is there to guide the boy into this vocation, even if the divine message is one of difficult words for his own family.

In this exchange, Eli also learns anew that God is merciful. After failing to rein in Hophni and Phinehas, God allows Eli to try again, to be a father in faith to this pure and gifted child who actually hears God speaking to him. Perhaps Eli is called to fatherhood once again here, this time to raise a true prophet who will be able to call a people who have grown lax in their faith back to right relationship with God.

Speak Lord, your servant is listening. What an amazing, timeless lesson from a humbled servant of God and a young prophet to be. The way Samuel and Eli find this lesson together reminds us of the importance of community, of God's family, as the true context for encountering the Word.

My little girl is in the thick of toddlerhood. Lots of big feelings and dramatic conflicts fill our days, and boundaries are frequently tested. We are both learning to communicate better in this intense season of life. This is a natural process for her and a humbling and sanctifying one for me, the adult who should know better. I am grateful that the grace of God still finds us in the middle of it all. Recently, at the end of a stressful supermarket visit culminating in a near meltdown, I asked her, exasperated, "What is it that you *need*, honey?"

"I need kisses!" she sobbed. *Speak, Lord.*

In digital culture, we are in a space of constant conversation, on a 24/7 global scale. We are connected around this chatter, and at times the voices therein are quite loud and strong. A lot is being said, shared, produced, posted. Influencers measure their success by their commitment to producing content and sharing it frequently and widely. At the same time, we might pause and wonder how much value we put on listening in these spaces. When it comes to our public forums, do we follow models who not only produce but also listen? When and with whom do we *listen together* these days? Whenever we truly gather around content, whenever we value the perspectives of others, whenever we ask real questions of one another and engage in dialogue, we are on our way.

None of us are in this alone. And a listening, humble heart assures that we remain open to the Word through those around us—the young, the old, the influential, the marginalized, even the disgraced.

We do our best listening together, especially in digital spaces.

PONDER: Who have been the guides into God's Word in my life? Have there been any unexpected guides? What have I learned while *listening together* with another?

PRAY: God of the Prophets, Your Divine Word sometimes comes at unexpected times and in unexpected places. At these times we rely on the community of faith to help us make sense of what you call us to do. Give us the listening ear of Samuel and the wise, humbled heart of Eli so we can be more attentive to your Word. Convert our hearts so we too can say, "Speak Lord, your servant is listening," and allow this to be the guiding statement of our lives of discipleship. We ask this through Jesus Christ, the Divine Word made flesh, by the power of the Holy Spirit, bearer of your Divine Wisdom. Amen.

9

A Light Silent Sound

(1 Kings 19:7-13a)

STATIO: Become still in body and mind. Take a minute to breathe and be aware of the moment.

LISTEN: What word or phrase stands out to you?

The angel of the LORD came back a second time, touched [Elijah], and said, "Get up and eat or the journey will be too much for you!" He got up, ate, and drank; then strengthened by that food, he walked forty days and forty nights to the mountain of God, Horeb.

There he came to a cave, where he took shelter. But the word of the LORD came to him: Why are you here, Elijah? He answered: "I have been most zealous for the LORD, the God of hosts, but the Israelites have forsaken your covenant. They have destroyed your altars and murdered your prophets by the sword. I alone remain, and they seek to take my life." Then the LORD said: Go out and stand on the mountain before the LORD; the LORD will pass by. There was a strong and violent wind rending the mountains and crushing rocks before the LORD—but the LORD was not in the wind; after the wind, an earthquake—but the Lord *was not in the earthquake; after the earthquake, fire—but the* Lord *was not in the fire; after the fire, a light silent sound.*

When he heard this, Elijah hid his face in his cloak and went out and stood at the entrance of the cave.

The Word of the Lord.

REFLECT: When Elijah spends forty days and nights journeying to the mountain of Horeb, he is at a tough place in his life and ministry. He is in flight from Queen Jezebel, who is persecuting him for standing up against her and King Ahab for their idolatrous support of the worship of Baal. Elijah is exhausted, alone in the wilderness, and wants to give up. He prays for death. Angels come to minister to him, urging him to eat. He travels on and arrives at Horeb, where Moses received the Word of God (Exod 20; Deut 5). He shelters himself there, desperate for the Divine Word as well.

Here is a person who feels defeated in ministry, yearning for encouragement from God. But where is God? Elijah is trying to preserve true worship in Israel, and for this, he has to run for his life! Why doesn't Almighty God, *El Shaddai*, show divine power, rise up, and sweep away the false gods? We might imagine Elijah shouting from his soul these painful questions.

Our souls might shout similar questions today: Why doesn't our Mighty God simply obliterate evil? Sex traffickers? Drug dealers? School shooters? Corrupt and unchaste church leaders? How can God allow these to stand?

I have been zealous for you, Lord. Where are you in the midst of injustice and corruption? Why not blow these away with your power? So my soul shouts sometimes.

But God does not shout back. God is not in the strong and violent wind. Not in the earthquake. Not in the fire. Could God command these and more to wipe away all sinfulness from the world? Yes. But this is not the way God chooses to come to humankind.

Though he may hope for God to shout and roar, Elijah discerns God's presence in the whisper, a "light silent sound." A lesson for all of us, especially during our dark night, our time on Horeb. When we desire the Divine Word the most, we can be assured that God speaks, but we must have ears and hearts that listen.

We too can hear that light silent sound. It is in the mystery of Mary's womb, the coos of the infant of Bethlehem, the "Follow me" extended to the apostles, the weeping at Lazarus's death, the silence before Pilate, the "It is finished" on the cross, the "Peace be with you" of the resurrection. Subtle words of divine presence that call us to listen more, to lean in closer, instead of covering our ears from the mighty roar.

It is difficult for us to hear God's whisper if we do not have silence. Silence is esteemed by most spiritual traditions, including Christianity. In silence, we put ourselves in a posture of hospitality to the Word, and it becomes the ground of our encounter. To really be still and receive the Word, we need to cultivate silence. This is not an easy discipline. Sometimes the noise we allow in from the outside has a purpose, as it blocks out our own inner turmoil. Sometimes it is hard to be in the presence of our own soul shouting. Silence calls us to listen, make peace, and learn to live with ourselves.

It is perhaps in light of this inner battle that God comes in the whisper. This gentleness of the Word takes down the decibels of our inner shouting, like a parent who shushes and rocks a bawling child. God whispers so our soul will be pacified.

There is nothing like the thick silence that surrounds the small child who has just fallen asleep. This could be because the peace and stillness come as such a contrast to the otherwise exuberant, wiggly, chattering energy of a child, even minutes before they fall asleep. Once they are sleeping, the silence that comes is remarkable. I have spent many nights sitting by little beds, soaking in this thick silence, staying there a while even after they have fallen asleep. After long, busy days, this has often been balm for my soul, a sacred time and space.

I wonder about the gift of silence in digital culture. Like time spent with small children, the digital flow is fast-paced, energetic, and constantly chattering. Critics often warn that digital culture is so busy that we are coming across more information than we can possibly process. As a result, we resort to continuously skimming the surface while our attention becomes fragmented. Without moments of silence—holy, thick silence—the constant flow of information is exhausting. With silence, we can hone our ears to the whisper of life-giving words, even in the midst of the digital flow.

A powerful moment of holy, thick silence in digital culture that many of us experienced was Pope Francis's "Urbi et Orbi" address and prayer for the end of the coronavirus pandemic on March 27, 2020. Through the media, the world watched him pray alone in a dark, rainy, and deserted St. Peter's Square, encouraging the world to bring our fears and trust to Jesus. In those turbulent days of the pandemic, the world found holy silence in this remarkable gathering, a gathering of absence, a communion in isolation. Digital technology was integral to creating this moment. It also showed us that chatter is not the only way to signal real presence in this space.

May the Spirit continue to open up for us these ways of encounter, presence, and communion.

PONDER: What helps me listen in my prayer life? What are some quiet, subtle ways I have encountered the Word? How has God whispered in my life?

PRAY: Almighty and Powerful God, your Word came to Elijah in the wilderness, and you continue to faithfully extend your Word and Spirit to humankind, especially to those who yearn to hear it most. Give us ears to hear like Elijah so we can discern your presence in a whisper and draw encouragement from even that light silent sound. Allow us to grow in trust and understanding that your might and power are not always what we expect them to be. Sometimes you will whisper, and yet you remain our Sovereign Lord. We ask this through Christ our Lord, by the power of the Holy Spirit. Amen.

10

Filled with the Holy Spirit

(Luke 1:39-56)

STATIO: Become still in body and mind. Take a minute to breathe and be aware of the moment.

LISTEN: What word or phrase stands out to you?

During those days Mary set out and traveled to the hill country in haste to a town of Judah, where she entered the house of Zechariah and greeted Elizabeth. When Elizabeth heard Mary's greeting, the infant leaped in her womb, and Elizabeth, filled with the holy Spirit, cried out in a loud voice and said, "Most blessed are you among women, and blessed is the fruit of your womb. And how does this happen to me, that the mother of my Lord should come to me? For at the moment the sound of your greeting reached my ears, the infant in my womb leaped for joy. Blessed are you who believed that what was spoken to you by the Lord would be fulfilled."

And Mary said:

"My soul proclaims the greatness of the Lord;
my spirit rejoices in God my savior.

For he has looked upon his handmaid's lowliness;
behold, from now on will all ages call me blessed.
The Mighty One has done great things for me,
and holy is his name.
His mercy is from age to age
to those who fear him.
He has shown might with his arm,
dispersed the arrogant of mind and heart.
He has thrown down the rulers from their thrones
but lifted up the lowly.
The hungry he has filled with good things;
the rich he has sent away empty.
He has helped Israel his servant,
remembering his mercy,
according to his promise to our fathers,
to Abraham and to his descendants forever."

Mary remained with her about three months and then returned to her home.

The Gospel of the Lord.

REFLECT: Mary has just met the angel Gabriel and offered her *yes* in response to God's invitation. She is pregnant with the Word and filled with the life of the Spirit. She sets out, and her visit to Elizabeth occurs immediately after this remarkable event. As Christian faithful, we are all called in some way to carry and share God's Word and Spirit with the world, and to reveal his Good News to all around us. But in Mary, this call takes form in an unprecedented, miraculous, and most embodied way. She actually carries the Word incarnate in her body and gives life to him for the life of the world.

A woman filled with the Spirit and carrying the Word. What did she sound like? What did she say? How did the living Word incarnate in her body shape her words and her communication? The event of the Visitation tells us.

First, it is remarkable that Word and Spirit *move her*. She sets out immediately and travels to see Elizabeth, to both witness and share the Good News of God's grace moving in human history. When she arrives, we are told that her words have a remarkable effect. The sound of her greeting moves Elizabeth and moves the infant joyfully in her body. Receiving Mary's word, Elizabeth in turn is filled with the Spirit and cries out in wonder and praise, recognizing the blessing of God upon her young cousin. Mary's words move Elizabeth to utter Spirit-filled words herself, words of blessing and praise. Elizabeth recognizes Mary as the Mother of her Lord.

Mother of my Lord. How does one possibly respond to that? Here is where we find the first actual words from Mary in Scripture after Word and Spirit have come upon her. And they are strong, faithful words that proclaim the greatness of God. *My soul proclaims the greatness of the Lord. My spirit rejoices in God my savior.* It is as if the Word himself is speaking through her, recalling God's great deeds and entrusting all to God moving forward. It is a profound prayer, an exemplary act of faith, a prayer that continues to resound in the church, generation after generation. We would expect nothing less from the sound of the Incarnate Word stirring within the body of the Virgin of Nazareth.

Do Word and Spirit resound today in digital culture? In a world where Zoom meetings and telepresence have become ordinary, Mary's deeply embodied experience with the Word calls us to reflection. Can we muster that fullness of presence, that total receptivity and gift of self to another that we see in the Incarnation? This was a presence that filled not only Mary but also Elizabeth, John the Baptist, and anyone else open to the Divine Word. How are we present to one another when so often these days the words we receive are mediated by a screen?

Telepresence was a significant feature of the COVID quarantine experience. Many of us held on to hope and joy during that difficult time by remaining connected to the world through our devices. My friends and I used a messaging app to send recorded videos back and forth. These videos of my friends sharing glimpses of their lives was a gift of their presence to me in those days. I will also never forget the videos of people singing from balconies or students holding up thank-you signs for their teachers on Zoom screens. During that fearful time of isolation, we found ways to be more present to one another with the help of technology. *My soul proclaims the greatness of the Lord.*

In the daily prayer of the church, we recite Mary's words during each day's Evening Prayer. Could this prayer guide us to be faithful communicators of God's Word and Spirit? Could Mary's words teach us to receive the Spirit, to bear the Word, and to proclaim God's greatness?

PONDER: What does the prayer of the *Magnificat* mean to me? What can Mary teach me through her words?

PRAY: Father of the Incarnate Word, you sent your Son into the world by the *fiat*, the "yes," of a young virgin, who was willingly overshadowed by your Spirit to welcome your Word. Since then, Mary has become our teacher in faith. Transform us by your grace so our hearts and minds may be transformed in her immaculate image, especially as faithful communicators of your Word and Spirit. May our souls magnify your greatness as we seek her intercession. Amen.

11

A Voice Cries Out in the Desert

(Matthew 3:1-8)

STATIO: Become still in body and mind. Take a minute to breathe and be aware of the moment.

LISTEN: What word or phrase stands out to you?

In those days John the Baptist appeared, preaching in the desert of Judea [and] saying, "Repent, for the kingdom of heaven is at hand!" It was of him that the prophet Isaiah had spoken when he said:

"A voice of one crying out in the desert,
'Prepare the way of the Lord,
make straight his paths.' "

John wore clothing made of camel's hair and had a leather belt around his waist. His food was locusts and wild honey. At that time Jerusalem, all Judea, and the whole region around the Jordan were going out to him and were being baptized by him in the Jordan River as they acknowledged their sins.

When he saw many of the Pharisees and Sadducees coming to his baptism, he said to them, "You brood of vipers!

Who warned you to flee from the coming wrath? Produce good fruit as evidence of your repentance."

The Gospel of the Lord.

REFLECT: From such a vivid description in Scripture, we can imagine John as a remarkable character. He is a wild man drawing a crowd to the desert, transforming hearts with raw, powerful, urgent words. I imagine him shouting, using big gestures and strong language. As far as faith communication goes, he was probably hard to miss.

Given this loud and passionate image of John, it may seem puzzling that the Christian tradition considers and reveres him as the original monastic. We picture monastics as calm and humble, measured in speech and unlikely to be shouting strong language. What then of John's strong words crying out in the desert? In what way is John exemplary for a spiritual tradition called to esteem silence and carefully chosen words? What about our strong words, our heated conversations today? Do these find a legitimate role and purpose in faithful communication?

John was a prophet, a servant of the Word, in the tradition of the Old Testament prophets before him. Biblical prophets served by helping the community recall God's Word and by offering guidance about how to return to right relationship with God. Passionate, urgent, tough-love words were often part of the task, but never without guidance back to God. The overall spirit of the prophet's words is constructive, building hope and possibility and right relationship with God. Statements like "brood of vipers," for example, is coupled with the directive to "produce good fruit."

Can our faithful words cry out in the desert? The desert, a place of stillness but also a site of struggle, sometimes needs voices that cry out, voices that blast the truth and clarity of God's Word in a way that cuts through the nonsense around us.

Simply blasting out words of faith does not, however, produce faithful communication. These days on social media platforms it takes little effort to blast anything out widely and instantly. As often happens, some time ago two prominent Catholic voices got into a heated exchange on Twitter (X). Their debate escalated to name-calling. Even though they both made thought-provoking points early on, what I continue to recall from their debate is the ugly words and personal attacks. Strongly worded comments about the faith, or present-day "brood of vipers" statements are not necessarily prophetic. Instead, what John and the prophets teach us about faith communication is the commitment to use words to guide the community back to God, and to offer a path for doing so. A prophet's words elevate the spirit, even through tough love.

PONDER: When do I feel the urge to "cry out in the desert" about the faith? What about the faith invites a strong reaction from me? How can a strong voice elevate the spirit?

PRAY: God of the Prophets, you call those who serve your Word to both courage to speak the truth, and compassion to guide others back to right relationship with you. Bless us with voices that cry out in the desert, and with the wisdom to use strong words for healing, reconciling, guiding, and building community. May the truth we speak always communicate hope and possibility. We ask this through Christ, by the power of the Spirit. Amen.

12

The Word Became Flesh

(John 1:1-5, 14)

STATIO: Become still in body and mind. Take a minute to breathe and be aware of the moment.

LISTEN: What word or phrase stands out to you?

In the beginning was the Word,
and the Word was with God,
and the Word was God.
He was in the beginning with God.
All things came to be through him,
and without him nothing came to be.
What came to be through him was life,
and this life was the light of the human race;
the light shines in the darkness,
and the darkness has not overcome it. . . .

And the Word became flesh
and made his dwelling among us,
and we saw his glory,
the glory as of the Father's only Son,
full of grace and truth.

The Gospel of the Lord.

REFLECT: *The Word was God.* Of all the divine metaphors and images within our tradition, the image of God as "Word" comes to us from the Gospel of John. The Word, as divine reason and intellect expressed in communication, reveals God. It is integral to who God is. In being Word and uttering the Word to humankind, ours is a God who communicates, and who does so from the beginning. In the Word, God always and already extends God's will and relationship.

Recalling God's "Let there be" at the moments of creation, here we ponder further the fact that God does not just *express* the Word but *identifies with* the Word. The mystery before us here is that there is something ultimate, something fundamental, in the substance and act of divine communication. What does this mean for our communication, done in faith?

Through the Word, we learn that communication is an act of simultaneously informing and relating with another. It is a movement toward another, a movement of both expression and receptivity, an intimacy and a communion. The Word becoming flesh tells us about divine closeness and, in turn, calls us to closeness. The Word builds community.

The Word of God is that through which all creation came to be. Life comes from the Word. Light comes from the Word. Awareness of the glory of God comes from the Word. Truly, the Word of God is the medium of God's activity, presence, and will. We discern this in the life, light, and glory that we discern in God's Word addressing us.

With this Prologue to his Gospel, John invites us into the awesome mystery of the Divine Word. For Christians, this is not only a mystery to ponder, it is a life to live. Don't just recognize the Divine Word, *listen* to it. Don't just behold God's light, *hurry away from the darkness*. Don't just appreciate these ultimate realities, *receive them into your heart* and *let them transform you*. The image of God as Word implies communication with us, and communication calls us into a dynamic experience. When the Word addresses us, we are not left the same.

There are words in our lives that have transformative power: *I am sorry. Forgive me. I love you.* From our history, we also honor unforgettable words that changed us: *I have a dream. One small step for man, one giant leap for mankind. In spite of everything I still believe that people are really good at heart.* When reflecting on our most powerful words, these too bring life, light, and a sense of transcendence and glory. Communication is a profound aspect of the human experience. From the perspective of faith, it is also an aspect that reveals God.

Made in the image of God and bound intimately to the Word who became flesh for us, how might we shape our words of faith? Life, light, and glory can be guiding beacons for this question. Do my words give life to another, show hope and possibility, offer encouragement and joy? Do my words offer light? Do they clarify, enlighten, and express truth? Do my words reveal God's glory, in substance and in relationship? Is my content of faith consistent with the manner in which I express it? Life, light, and glory can guide our communication toward the activity of the Divine Word.

Life, light, and glory are also a discernment point these days, as digital culture is increasingly populated by artificial intelligence (AI). This raises profound questions for faith. If we are made in God's image, in whose image is artificial intelligence? Is AI an entity of sorts or just a very effective program? How might we view or understand an AI-made text or artwork, a deepfake video, or chatbots? Is coming across these an encounter? Do they convey a sense of presence? In a recent conversation I led about spirituality and digital culture, someone raised this challenging and thoughtful question: *Are we called to engage AI with the same hospitality and dignity that we should extend to persons?* What if we do not know whether our encounter is in fact with a person or with AI? How do we morally approach that?

In some ways, it does not matter if our communication partner happens to be an AI. Life, light, and glory, gifts of the Divine Word, should imbue our communication across the board. What matters is our disposition, our gift of self, whether the engagement is with a chatbot or a human. Even if we are engaging with a chatbot, our communication becomes occasion for witness in the public forum of the internet and an ongoing reflection of our faithfulness to the Divine Word.

PONDER: Life, light, and glory. How can each of these inspire my communication practices today?

PRAY: God in Mystery, your Word reveals you from the beginning. In Jesus Christ, the Word Incarnate, you communicated yourself to humankind so we may arrive, through your life, light, and glory, at eternal communion with you. Grant us words that are ever faithful to the Word, shape our communication after Christ, in both content and the manner of our lives. We ask this through the Incarnate Word, by the power of the Spirit. Amen.

13

Who Do You Say That I Am?

(Matthew 16:13-17)

STATIO: Become still in body and mind. Take a minute to breathe and be aware of the moment.

LISTEN: What word or phrase stands out to you?

When Jesus went into the region of Caesarea Philippi he asked his disciples, "Who do people say that the Son of Man is?" They replied, "Some say John the Baptist, others Elijah, still others Jeremiah or one of the prophets." He said to them, "But who do you say that I am?" Simon Peter said in reply, "You are the Messiah, the Son of the living God." Jesus said to him in reply, "Blessed are you, Simon son of Jonah. For flesh and blood has not revealed this to you, but my heavenly Father."

The Gospel of the Lord.

REFLECT: *Who do you say that I am?* This question of Jesus directed at the disciples is a phrase in the Bible that leaps off the page. Sitting with this—*really* sitting with this—presents a compelling encounter with the Living Word. *You, child of*

God in the twenty-first century, who do you say that I am? This question rouses and invites a faith response, then and now.

Held within this question is a fundamental assumption about faith communication: that the disciple of Jesus communicates who Jesus is. Jesus does not ask *if* we will say who he is, but assumes that we should do so. Instead, he seeks the core of our message about him.

Jesus as the Incarnate Word revealed God in his person. This means that not only his words and preaching but his very being, his presence in the community, communicated God. This also means that Jesus, in the way he shared his life with the people, was never *not* communicating God. This is an important lesson for faith communication. First, we are all called to communicate who Jesus is and find our authentic, truthful voice for doing so. Beyond repetition of content, this calls for a true statement of faith. Who do I know Jesus to be in my heart of hearts? How have I encountered him and learned who he is? Jesus' question does not have a quick answer. It is an invitation to prayer and reflection before articulating a precious response, a confession of faith. Peter's "You are the Messiah, the Son of the living God" is one of the most profound utterances of his life.

Seeking to recognize the presence of Christ, especially in unexpected places, is one of the hallmarks of Christian spirituality. The Gospel of Matthew reminds us that this is not always an easy or comfortable task. Christ is in the marginalized, the poor, the "other," those considered undesirable by society (Matt 25:31-46). "Welcoming the stranger as Christ" is a collective term for this disposition that we inherit from the wisdom of Christian monastics. According to monastic practice, when a stranger comes to the monastery, they are received as Christ, welcomed with a bow, and are invited to pray together to be "united in peace" (see, for example, the Rule of St. Benedict 53).

In Peter's proclamation of Jesus as the Messiah, it is as if he is recognizing Jesus as the Christ (the Greek equivalent of "Messiah") for the first time. Peter's recognition of Christ leads him to a confession, a powerful prayer statement expressing his faith. Like the monastics welcoming Christ in the stranger, Peter too is uttering words of prayer as he welcomes Christ. And like the stranger showing up at the monastery, it is Jesus' prompting with the question, "Who do you say that I am?" which initiates this revelatory encounter.

Like the stranger who arrives unbidden, Jesus always is present first and calls us into encounter and relationship. We too are presented with his question "Who do you say that I am?" We may profess our faith like Peter. We also express who we believe Jesus is by the way we share our lives with other people. Here we are also called to prayerful reflection—less about making a confessional statement of faith, and more about bringing awareness to how our manner of life is consistent with that same confession. We say who Jesus is in our kindness, hospitality, patience, encouragement, and more. When we are lacking in these, when our confession of faith is inconsistent with our manner of life, this invites scrutiny and scandal.

If we are not attentive to *the way* we communicate with others, social media comment feeds can become a battlefield around topics of faith or theology. Imagine for a moment if a person entirely unfamiliar with the Christian tradition gained his or her impression of it solely from what Christians are posting on Twitter (X). Would they gain a sense of the Gospel, or would they instead perceive deep polarization and the hanging threat of schism? Attacking others, mocking them sarcastically for their points of view, is sadly a matter of course these days on our social media platforms. Just like in a battle, people gather in "camps" over against those "others" whose understanding of the tradition is "heresy." Weaponized words create division in the social media arena, fomenting animosity toward other people of faith, other brothers and sisters in Christ, or even the stranger who might be Christ in disguise.

In addition to the lack of charity toward fellow Christians, we also project a broken, shattered image of community though this kind of behavior. If faithful communication builds communion, divisive and hurtful communication accomplishes the opposite. Convicted by the Spirit who gathers us in, we are called back to the question of Jesus: *Who do you say that I am?*

PONDER: How do I respond to the question, "Who do you say that I am?" Who do I say that Jesus is explicitly? Who do I say that Jesus is by manner of my presence? Are these consistent with each another?

PRAY: God of Communion, through your Word and Spirit, you invite us to communicate our faith in word and manner of life. Your Son calls us to state our faith not only as a confession but as an embodied expression lived in daily life. Inspire us to live from our true encounter with Jesus and share the joy of this encounter with the world. Give us the words to articulate our faith and the wisdom and perseverance to embody it day to day. We ask this through Christ the Teacher, by the power of the Spirit. Amen.

14

The Sheep Hear His Voice

(John 10:1-5, 14)

STATIO: Become still in body and mind. Take a minute to breathe and be aware of the moment.

LISTEN: What word or phrase stands out to you?

"Amen, amen, I say to you, whoever does not enter a sheepfold through the gate but climbs over elsewhere is a thief and a robber. But whoever enters through the gate is the shepherd of the sheep. The gatekeeper opens it for him, and the sheep hear his voice, as he calls his own sheep by name and leads them out. When he has driven out all his own, he walks ahead of them, and the sheep follow him, because they recognize his voice. But they will not follow a stranger; they will run away from him, because they do not recognize the voice of strangers. . . . I am the good shepherd, and I know mine and mine know me."

The Gospel of the Lord.

REFLECT: The Good Shepherd image is an ancient one for Christians. From the early days of the church, this image for

Christ has spoken profoundly of Christ's care, guidance, protection, and limitless love for his followers. Significant for our reflection on communication is the fact that the bond between the shepherd and the sheep is established by the sheep hearing and knowing the shepherd's voice. The relationship of care, trust, guidance, and protection is built on the familiarity of the voice of the shepherd. It is a relationship built on communication, on listening to and trusting the voice of another.

The sheep follow the shepherd because they listen to his voice. Deeper than just a comfortable familiarity with a voice that is "often around," the sheep know the shepherd's voice because he actually calls them by name. The shepherd's voice is personal. Intimate. It doesn't just resound in the sheepfold's ambience, it *addresses them directly*. Obedient to this voice, the sheep are led to safety, nourishment, and life.

Obedience is a complex word for our culture today. It carries a connotation of one overpowering another. To obey seems to mean being disempowered and "less than" as another person or entity exerts their more powerful will.

Obedience is a concept worth rescuing from this power-laden definition. It is actually a term that is deeply rooted both in spirituality and in communication. The common Latin roots of *audire* (to listen) and *obaudire* (to listen to, to obey) have wisdom for us. From this shared connection, to obey implies the kind of listening that is relationally directed, that offers hospitality to the word of another. Obedience puts the act of listening in the context of a relationship. So fundamental is this to living well in community that the monastic Rule of Benedict asserts that "it is by this way of obedience that we go to God" (RB 71.2).

This wisdom from the Rule is certainly true for the sheep. They listen to (obey) the voice of the shepherd who leads them to life. They listen to him because they have been addressed by him, each called by name. Christ addresses each of us, calls us to relationship. In turn, as we step into that relationship, we are formed by it to relate with others in the same manner. Obedience is a gesture of relating trustingly with the one who calls us by name. It is a familiarity born out of relationship.

Reflecting on this passage raises the question for our time of how to hear the voice of the shepherd, how to become attentive to it, and how to recognize being called by name. In digital culture, so many voices are present, seeking our attention. The number of daily marketing emails in our inboxes and targeted ads before us on social media are just one symptom of a world full of voices addressing us. Like predatory wolves, misinformation, scams, and phishing messages lurk. Beyond this we find more personal voices, passionately presenting this opinion or that. What is true and who to follow? Which of these voices lead us to life? It seems all the more important these days to recognize the voice of the shepherd, for the same guidance, protection, and life promised to the flock.

In recent years many professional settings have started offering information technology safety trainings. Our version at my university comes as a monthly instructional video coupled with a brief quiz. Most agree that regular training like this offers important and valuable skills for navigating digital contexts discerningly and prudently, and in a way that protects sensitive data. Good training teaches us to avoid the digital data wolves, clad in sheep's clothing.

In digital culture, data is not the only thing worth protecting. From the perspective of faith, we have the sense that the influx of so much information, the clamoring of so many voices, has a spiritual impact on us. It can be hard to recognize the good, the true, and the life-giving. If we have realized the importance of training in the professional world, we might also reflect on how to prepare our spirits to be more discerning in this cacophonous context. We need training for the ear of our hearts, to hear the shepherd's voice.

Seeking familiarity with his voice is a call to spiritual practice. It is a call to spend time in prayer with the Word, to experience being addressed by name, to be held by God's gentle wisdom and loving presence. In these spaces, we come to know the shepherd's voice. Knowing this voice shapes us, compels us to follow and to live in a way that reflects the one we know. This intimacy also gives life to our own communication, the way we may call others by name and into truth, life, and communion by the way we use our words.

PONDER: In what ways have I recognized the Shepherd's voice? What helps me bring my attention to his call? How does knowing his voice shape the way I call out to others?

PRAY: Loving Father, you sent your Son the Good Shepherd to calls us by name, to communicate to us your love and invitation to life. Bless us with your Spirit's wisdom to be able to continue to discern his voice, and empower us with the clarity and courage to obey and follow his lead, both in our own communication and in the way we live our lives. We ask this in the name of Christ, the Good Shepherd, who knows us and whom we know. Amen.

15

Moved with Compassion

(Luke 10:29-37)

STATIO: Become still in body and mind. Take a minute to breathe and be aware of the moment.

LISTEN: What word or phrase stands out to you?

But because he [a scholar of the law] wished to justify himself, he said to Jesus, "And who is my neighbor?" Jesus replied, "A man fell victim to robbers as he went down from Jerusalem to Jericho. They stripped and beat him and went off leaving him half-dead. A priest happened to be going down that road, but when he saw him, he passed by on the opposite side. Likewise a Levite came to the place, and when he saw him, he passed by on the opposite side. But a Samaritan traveler who came upon him was moved with compassion at the sight. He approached the victim, poured oil and wine over his wounds and bandaged them. Then he lifted him up on his own animal, took him to an inn and cared for him. The next day he took out two silver coins and gave them to the innkeeper with the instruction, 'Take care of him. If you spend more than what I have given you, I shall repay you on my way back.' Which of these three, in your opinion, was neighbor to the robbers' victim?" He answered, "The one who treated him with mercy." Jesus said to him, "Go and do likewise."

The Gospel of the Lord.

REFLECT: The parable of the Good Samaritan is a story about compassion, healing, and building community. It is a profound reflection on relating well with others. In the Catholic tradition, it has also been held up as an icon for reflecting on the challenges of digital culture and communication.[1] In this vein, it is also a communication story.

We can picture the actions of the Samaritan clearly in our minds. How did his communication feature in the care and mercy he extended to the victim of roadside robbery? It is easy to imagine some of his words upon finding the victim: "Are you conscious? Can I help you? Can you hear me? Who did this to you?" But the parable does not register these. Instead, the first word we hear from the Samaritan, a simple and brief directive to the innkeeper, is an invitation to compassion: "Take care of him." Though a seemingly minor player in the narrative, the innkeeper is traditionally held to be a symbol for the church. In directing the only spoken words of the Samaritan (himself an allegory for Christ) to the innkeeper, Jesus makes it clear that this story is an invitation to compassion, closeness, and tenderness to all who would follow him.

[1] See the 2023 pastoral reflection from the Dicastery for Communication, "Towards Full Presence." This document uses the parable of the Good Samaritan as its overarching theme to inspire faithful communication in social media contexts.

Closeness, compassion, and tenderness are three ways to characterize the action of the Good Samaritan, and they have been held up as imperative for shaping our presence and communication in digital culture.[2] In many ways, digital spaces are like the Jericho road. They are dynamic spaces, a necessary path to walk these days, but one that can also be perilous. The robbers lurking in these spaces are aplenty: robbers of our attention, robbers of our time, robbers of our sense of truth and moderation. Robbers may thieve us of our focus and clarity. They may inflict us with violent words or a lack of regard for basic human dignity and decency toward others. This context cries out for Good Samaritans, agents who are willing to look past the trappings of digital culture and remain insistent on expressing our shared humanity therein. Agents of closeness, compassion, and tenderness who insist on the value of human encounter in digital spaces and practice listening well, being present especially to brokenness, and extending care to those who are wounded.

Good Samaritans do not work alone. The Good Samaritan invites collaboration from the innkeeper and begins to form community around the victim who was left battered and utterly alone. This impetus to gather, to form and deepen social bonds in a way that aims toward communion, is essential to communicating well in digital culture. However we share our words in digital spaces, they ought to be words that accompany, heal, and gather community.

[2] Often referring to closeness, compassion, and tenderness as "God's style," Pope Francis has offered frequent reflections on this theme. See, for example, "Towards Full Presence," 64.

I have worked closely with church ministers for many years, and I appreciate the wisdom they bring to my classroom. From them I have often heard stories of people calling the church office, needing support and a listening ear in a way that extends well beyond the practical job description of the minister answering the call. In this way, wounded strangers appear and invite ministers to be like the Good Samaritan, to stop long enough to listen to painful stories, to offer words that are wine and balm for the soul, and to be a compassionate and welcoming presence that might lead a wounded soul back to community. All this unfolds through intentional, faithful communication. The good minister has an ear rooted in the heart to pick up on the importance of these conversations and to stop, though they could easily cross the road and keep going.

However we may find someone battered by the side of the road, our primary response to such a one is compassion. Compassion is integral to being community; without compassion we are unable to build relationships with others. Especially when it comes to estranged members of a community, compassion is fundamental for restoring these relationships. Like the balm and wine of the Good Samaritan that he pours on the wounds of the victim, extending compassion through presence, listening, and empathy can offer life and hope to even the most heartbroken. In the case of faithful communication, it is often our words and gestures themselves that are the balm and wine for someone's wounds. Even the way we answer the phone or look up when someone walks in matters. In the digital realm, when our inboxes are inundated and we skim and skip to stay on top of them, simply reading and thoughtfully responding to a person's message in a timely way can be a gesture of presence and compassion.

Community is built on compassion, and the spirit of compassion is especially inclusive of those most in need of healing and mercy.

PONDER: Who have I encountered wounded by the side of the road in digital contexts? What might compassionate communication look like?

PRAY: God of Infinite Love, your Son embodied for us your compassion, closeness, and tenderness in word and deed. Like the Good Samaritan calling forth the innkeeper, he tells us to take care of one another in the same spirit. Make us attentive to those left wounded by the side of the road, and help us to be mindful of compassionate communication as a way to bring healing to wounds, especially those sustained in digital spaces. We ask this in the name of your Son Jesus, by the power of the Holy Spirit. Amen.

16

Lazarus, Come Out

(John 11:38-45)

STATIO: Become still in body and mind. Take a minute to breathe and be aware of the moment.

LISTEN: What word or phrase stands out to you?

So Jesus, perturbed again, came to the tomb. It was a cave, and a stone lay across it. Jesus said, "Take away the stone." Martha, the dead man's sister, said to him, "Lord, by now there will be a stench; he has been dead for four days." Jesus said to her, "Did I not tell you that if you believe you will see the glory of God?" So they took away the stone. And Jesus raised his eyes and said, "Father, I thank you for hearing me. I know that you always hear me; but because of the crowd here I have said this, that they may believe that you sent me." And when he had said this, he cried out in a loud voice, "Lazarus, come out!" The dead man came out, tied hand and foot with burial bands, and his face was wrapped in a cloth. So Jesus said to them, "Untie him and let him go."

Now many of the Jews who had come to Mary and seen what he had done began to believe in him.

The Gospel of the Lord.

REFLECT: Jesus raising Lazarus is one of the most dramatic scenes of the Gospels. It is a powerful event that brings together elements of love, loss and grief, faith and trust, humanity and divinity, life and death. In the story of Lazarus we witness both the power of God as well as the tender humanity of Jesus.

After four days dead in the tomb, Lazarus is raised to life by Jesus. The power of God is clear and active. Manifesting that power, Jesus could have used any number of ways to restore the life of his friend. It is significant that the "method" Jesus chooses to restore life is a communicative act. He cries out in a loud voice and commands the dead Lazarus back to life. His loud cry here recalls his preaching earlier in the Gospel: "The hour is coming in which all who are in the tombs *will hear [the Son of Man's] voice* and will come out, those who have done good deeds to the resurrection of life, but those who have done wicked deeds to the resurrection of condemnation" (John 5:28-29, emphasis mine). Here, the Word of God present at creation is manifest once again as this time, life is restored by the Word. We are invited to witness life-giving divine presence through the lens of communication. Jesus turns to the Father and praises the Father for hearing him. Father and Son are in communication; they *are* communication. Overflowing from the mutual gift of self that exists between the Father and the Son, Jesus' life-giving words to Lazarus pour out: "Lazarus, come out." The dead man stirs to life. And Martha, Mary, the crowd, and the rest of us stand in awe at the life-giving power of the Divine Word.

Attentiveness to the life-giving power of God's Word is fundamental for our life in Christ. This attentiveness is more than just an awareness. It is meant to rouse us, put us in motion. The Word of God is meant to animate us to abundant life. This is especially powerful at those times when we suffer from the deadening weight of apathy, meaninglessness, or despair.

Being attuned to the voice of Christ is essential. As those rising from the tomb remind us, our very lives depend on it. From the "Let there be" of creation to the calling forth of the entombed dead, the Word of God is life.

I will never forget the day I heard the heartbreaking news that a former student, who later became a priest, took his own life. He was a generous person, life-giving with his hospitality and encouragement of others, including me, his newly appointed professor at the time. Some years later, our last exchange occurred via social media. I posted news of a new professional appointment, and he commented: "Go and be awesome." Knowing he was aware of my professional journey and its ups and downs, I smiled and took to heart his comment. Still encouraging, his last words to me gave me life. I pray for the repose of his soul. As his words gave life to many, may the life-giving Word raise him to eternal life.

Digital culture calls forth our words. To be present in digital spaces, we share our words in text, sound, and image in order to animate the network with human interaction. In many ways, our words give the network its life. What an awesome, rousing thought! Whether we intend it or not, our genuine communication finds itself rooted in the life-giving dynamic of the Divine Word. How well we live this out, how deeply we allow our communication to take root in this sacred foundation, is up to us.

Our words animate and bring presence to digital networks. What kind of presence ought we shape that to be? How might it not just animate connections but genuinely bring life? What might our life-giving words look like? Life-giving words are rousing words, words of light that illuminate the darkness of the tomb and bring freedom to loosen the constraints that bind us. Life-giving words call us forth, give direction toward life, love, and community. Life-giving words offer second chances, hope, restoration. Life-giving words resurrect and fill the heart so that it will share its love with others.

PONDER: In what ways is my heart hardened to the life-giving Word of God? How might my words be life-giving to others? What does it mean for me to offer a rousing word?

PRAY: God of Life, your Son's resounding Word restored life to Lazarus and brought him forth from the tomb to love and community. We await your Son's same life-giving Word to call us all to eternal life. Rouse us with your Word today so we might recognize our communication as rooted in the Word, and so we may also be intentional about our words as calling forth life, hope, and love in others, especially those who feel entombed in spirit. We pray this in the name of Jesus Christ, by the power of the Holy Spirit. Amen.

17

What Is Truth?

(John 18:28-40)

STATIO: Become still in body and mind. Take a minute to breathe and be aware of the moment.

LISTEN: What word or phrase stands out to you?

Then they brought Jesus from Caiaphas to the praetorium. It was morning. And they themselves did not enter the praetorium, in order not to be defiled so that they could eat the Passover. So Pilate came out to them and said, "What charge do you bring [against] this man?" They answered and said to him, "If he were not a criminal, we would not have handed him over to you." At this, Pilate said to them, "Take him yourselves, and judge him according to your law." The Jews answered him, "We do not have the right to execute anyone," in order that the word of Jesus might be fulfilled that he said indicating the kind of death he would die. So Pilate went back into the praetorium and summoned Jesus and said to him, "Are you the King of the Jews?" Jesus answered, "Do you say this on your own or have others told you about me?" Pilate answered, "I am not a Jew, am I? Your own nation and the chief priests handed you over to me. What have you done?" Jesus answered, "My kingdom does not belong to this world. If my kingdom did belong to this world, my attendants [would] be fighting to keep me from being handed over to the Jews. But as it is, my kingdom is not here." So Pilate said to him, "Then you are a king?" Jesus answered, "You say I am a king. For this I was born and for this I came into the world, to testify to the truth. Everyone who belongs to the truth listens to my voice." Pilate said to him, "What is truth?"

When he had said this, he again went out to the Jews and said to them, "I find no guilt in him. But you have a custom that I release one prisoner to you at Passover. Do you want me to release to you the King of the Jews?" They cried out again, "Not this one but Barabbas!" Now Barabbas was a revolutionary.

The Gospel of the Lord.

REFLECT: Pilate is a man who suffers under the decision between doing the right thing and doing the popular thing. He is an ambiguous character who seems almost convinced to do the right thing but then fails at the last minute.

What is truth? This is perhaps Pilate's most famous line in the Gospels. We wonder how he said it: genuinely, cynically, curiously, dismissively, rhetorically, mockingly? Was he *really* asking Jesus? Or was he speaking to himself? It is all open to interpretation, and plenty of Jesus films have interpreted this scene in unique ways to show different sides of Pilate. On some level we are encouraged that he asks it, perhaps as a glimmer of recognition of the Son of Man standing before him. But we are left disappointed when, instead of waiting for an answer, instead of listening to Jesus respond, he follows his own question with walking away.

Pilate walks away from seeking the truth. When he turns to the crowd, his actions demonstrate this. He makes a true statement ("I find no guilt in him"), but he does not act on that truth. This is a moral failure. As a result, he consents instead to falsehood, granting freedom to a well-known criminal. We understand his actions as succumbing to the pressure of the crowd and doing the popular thing.

Truthfulness is a characteristic rooted in communicative action. One *communicates* the truth in word and deed in order *to be truthful* with another person. In truthfulness, communication expresses our interior life and connects us with those around us. Truthfulness is essential for healthy and authentic relationships, and for integrity in faith. Truthfulness is also the building block of community. If we cannot trust the truthfulness of the word of another, we no longer listen. We part ways.

It is often the pressure of perceived social dynamics that tempt us away from truthfulness. We worry about how we come across, how the truth might bring out an adverse reaction in others. Like Pilate we too struggle with the influence of others, especially on social media. Such social dynamics are integral to digital culture. Take social media influencers, for example. Once built on the authenticity of people sharing their unfiltered opinions, influencing now has become a powerful and lucrative marketing strategy designed to push products. Because of the impact of the crowd, the influencer these days is more focused on selling than authentically relating. In the midst of this, the truth can be mitigated, watered down, or even compromised. Viewing an influencer's video, we may again wonder: *What is truth?*

How do we respond in faith to the powerful influence of others on social media? It is hard to stand by the truth when powerful popular voices claim things otherwise. It is also hard when the whole world seems to have decided on a scandalous, enraging verdict about the latest social issue within minutes. If we suggest waiting, seeking balance, or exploring another angle, we are labeled as part of the problem and receive the mockery and ire of the mob. Suddenly Pilate doesn't seem so weak anymore. We too get the pressure of the crowd.

Yet as the Vatican's recent reflection on social media encourages us, "We should all take our influence seriously. Every Christian is a micro-influencer."[1] Our "influence" depends not on likes, follows, and subscribes, but on our faithfulness to the Lord. In faith we see why the better teacher for us is the Lord himself, who is not afraid to face the crowd and take up his cross. His way changes the world. *Behold the man* (John 19:5).

PONDER: How can I stay faithful to the truth in the face of social pressure?

PRAY: Father of Our Lord, you sent your Son to reveal to us the way, the truth, and the life, and he does this most perfectly through the mystery of his passion, death, and resurrection.

[1] "Towards Full Presence," 74.

He teaches us how to remain faithful in the face of pressure, mockery, and violence, and to serve the truth with our words and witness. Give us your grace, that we too may be able to stand alongside him with steadfastness and conviction, especially when it comes to sharing your Good News. Grant this through Jesus Christ, by the power of the Holy Spirit. Amen.

18

Suddenly a Noise

(Acts 2:1-12)

STATIO: Become still in body and mind. Take a minute to breathe and be aware of the moment.

LISTEN: What word or phrase stands out to you?

When the time for Pentecost was fulfilled, they were all in one place together. And suddenly there came from the sky a noise like a strong driving wind, and it filled the entire house in which they were. Then there appeared to them tongues as of fire, which parted and came to rest on each one of them. And they were all filled with the holy Spirit and began to speak in different tongues, as the Spirit enabled them to proclaim.

Now there were devout Jews from every nation under heaven staying in Jerusalem. At this sound, they gathered in a large crowd, but they were confused because each one heard them speaking in his own language. They were astounded, and in amazement they asked, "Are not all these people who are speaking Galileans? Then how does each of us hear them in his own native language? We are Parthians, Medes, and Elamites, inhabitants of Mesopotamia, Judea and Cappadocia,

Pontus and Asia, Phrygia and Pamphylia, Egypt and the districts of Libya near Cyrene, as well as travelers from Rome, both Jews and converts to Judaism, Cretans and Arabs, yet we hear them speaking in our own tongues of the mighty acts of God." They were all astounded and bewildered, and said to one another, "What does this mean?"

The Word of the Lord.

REFLECT: The story of Pentecost is a communication story through and through. It begins with a listening stillness and deep anticipation. This is followed powerfully by the Spirit's arrival with sound and wind and tongues of fire. The Spirit brings the gift of the ability to speak the faith, which is then manifest in the miracle of languages and the declaration of the wonders of God to "devout Jews from every nation" who are in Jerusalem. This process—from prayerful listening, to receiving the gift the Spirit, to the joy of sharing the Gospel with others—encapsulates faithful communication.

It all begins in the Upper Room, a place of waiting, praying, listening, anticipating. The disciples have been told to wait for the promise of the Father (Acts 1:4), to wait for baptism by the Spirit (1:5). Did they know what was coming? Did they sit in ambiguity and perhaps even some apprehension? Did they harbor doubts? It is possible that the Upper Room held all of this and more while they listened for God. But they were there, and they were open, extending hospitality to the Spirit.

We may find ourselves in Upper Rooms when facing important and daunting conversations: Reaching out to someone we love who is in trouble. Offering an honest perspective to one who may or may not want to hear it. Opening our hearts and being vulnerable without knowing how this will be received or reciprocated. Before such conversations, we may sit in stillness, waiting for courage and wisdom, waiting for knowledge and understanding, waiting for these and other gifts of the Spirit to come and fill our doubts with conviction and move us forward. At Pentecost, these gifts came as sound and flaming tongues. We may also experience them as joy, hope, possibility, insight, or simply a stability of heart.

Stability is a deep sense of commitment. When we interiorize this commitment as a spiritual value, it becomes a rootedness, a firm foundation, a conviction within. In a dynamic and complex world, our inner stability is often the only place of stillness. There is immense joy in finding our footing this way, of standing firm in spirit, especially when all else can seem chaotic. This stability is our home.

In the Spirit we are given the ability to speak, and we are compelled to go out and share this joy, this stability, this hope and new life. It is remarkable that the Spirit arrives first of all with sound—and loud noise at that! I find it beautiful that there is such an abundance of sound coming to immerse in grace those disciples who have been waiting and praying in uncertainty. Here they are not discerning a whisper of the heart. Rather, the Spirit arrives powerfully, in a "can't miss it" sort of way, and pours out grace in the form of fiery tongues. Tongues, muscles for speech, but full of light, heat, power! In a most formidable way, the disciples are given the ability to communicate the faith: to declare the wonders of God, but also to have hard conversations, to stand up for truth and justice, to gather community and to give life with words, and, most fundamentally, to make a gift of themselves, offered in love through any act of communication. Whenever this occurs authentically, we find once again the Spirit blowing through our Upper Rooms.

Discovering Upper Room experiences in digital culture is integral for faithful communication. I will never forget March 13, 2013, the day Cardinal Jorge Bergoglio was elected pope. That day, in the midst of work commitments, I was following the progression of the conclave on Twitter (X). The spirit of the conclave on Twitter (X) was remarkable. People tweeting from St Peter's Square and from around the world gathered in joyful anticipation in that digital space. Their spirit was palpable as the hashtag #conclave became a gathering point, a place for updates and sharing. The atmosphere was positive, joyful, celebratory, full of life. It was sacred space, full of Spirit. I have not seen anything like it on Twitter (X) since.

The Spirit comes. But are we there for it? Abiding in the Upper Room is listening well, making room, looking outside of ourselves, welcoming the other, creating a space for hospitality, encounter, and community. Above all, it is attending to the joy and life the Spirit brings when we gather in faith. The Upper Room forms us to be faithful communicators.

PONDER: How might I envision my interior space as an Upper Room? What lessons does Pentecost hold for my interior life? How does the Spirit give me the ability to speak?

PRAY: God of Power and Might, you poured out your Spirit in the Upper Room of Pentecost to enflame the listening hearts of the disciples who awaited you there. Your Spirit continues to give us the breath, passion, and conviction to communicate our faith. Give us tongues aflame with the same passion and conviction so we too can communicate faith across boundaries, barriers, and divisions. May our words gather community by the power of your Spirit. We ask this in the name of Jesus Christ. Amen.

19

Follow the Spirit

(Galatians 5:16-26)

STATIO: Become still in body and mind. Take a minute to breathe and be aware of the moment.

LISTEN: What word or phrase stands out to you?

I say, then: live by the Spirit and you will certainly not gratify the desire of the flesh. For the flesh has desires against the Spirit, and the Spirit against the flesh; these are opposed to each other, so that you may not do what you want. But if you are guided by the Spirit, you are not under the law. Now the works of the flesh are obvious: immorality, impurity, licentiousness, idolatry, sorcery, hatreds, rivalry, jealousy, outbursts of fury, acts of selfishness, dissensions, factions, occasions of envy, drinking bouts, orgies, and the like. I warn you, as I warned you before, that those who do such things will not inherit the kingdom of God. In contrast, the fruit of the Spirit is love, joy, peace, patience, kindness, generosity, faithfulness, gentleness, self-control. Against such there is no law. Now those who belong to Christ [Jesus] have crucified their flesh with its passions and desires. If we live in the Spirit, let us also follow the Spirit. Let us not be conceited, provoking one another, envious of one another.

The Word of the Lord.

REFLECT: Word and Spirit are intimately connected in faith communication. God's Word is uttered since the beginning, and continues to give life to all that is. This same Word is carried forth by the breath of God's Spirit, moving the Word *to address* and *to relate* with all of creation. The Spirit firms the bonds of divine self-gift. The Spirit gathers and build community. The Spirit moves all that is toward communion. In the power of the Spirit, we become sharers of the Word. We become the Word's hearers and doers (Jas 1:22).

Appreciating the call to faithful communication, we will still wonder in countless circumstances: *What do I actually say?* When in digital spaces, we might ponder what to post, share, or comment so it abides in the same Spirit of God's life-giving Word. This is especially true in contentious conversations that we see in comment feeds. What does foolproof faithful content look like, content that brings light and life even to contentious contexts? The problem is that it is difficult to establish a formula for what effective faith communication looks like. God's Word is not formulaic but *living*. It addresses each and every heart and circumstance, in the mode of the hearer, and gently accompanies us toward communion. Still, we are tempted to wonder: *How might we capture this in a post?*

There is no formula for communicating faith. Likewise, there are no perfect apps, platforms, or formats for doing this in digital spaces. The question is not a technical one, anyway, but a spiritual one. To communicate faithfully, we must discern our foundation. We must determine where our ability to speak the faith comes from.

What we strive to say in faith ought, above all, to abide in the Spirit. If we follow the Spirit and learn to express ourselves accordingly, we are faithful communicators. Any content that is faithful flows from this fundamental relationship.

At the same time, the Spirit does not merely thrust us toward communion. God's Spirit accompanies, guides, and counsels along the way. While there is no one formula for communicating faith, the fruits of the Spirit can offer a litmus test of sorts for discerning the spirit of our words. Is what I offer loving? Peaceful? Joyful? Patient and kind? Generous, faithful? Gentle and self-controlled? Against such there is no law.

There is a humorous meme I often see on social media. The backdrop is a 1990s Chicago Bulls basketball game, and the meme pictures Michael Jordan pulling on the jersey of Dennis Rodman, holding him back from doing something impulsive or foolish. Clever content creators labeled Jordan "The Holy Spirit" and Rodman "My responses to people on social media." I smile at this meme, being thoroughly familiar with the impulse to launch some quick and cutting comment, to put someone "in their place." The Spirit has pulled my jersey, too, cautioning me to think twice when I am feeling this impulse.

More than just preserving us from foolishness or embarrassment, the Spirit moves in these circumstances for the sake of community. Fundamentally the impulse to cut someone down comes from pride, from the belief that our way is better. And the proud, self-serving person is antithetical to community life. The Spirit's caution is an invitation to humility, to hold back on dominating with what we think we have to offer, and instead to look for ways that build up. Spirit-led communication can make space, create a way, form bonds where there were no bonds. A gift of self that follows the Spirit likewise aims to make room and to receive others. Our own measured communication in this sense is an act of hospitality. It is communication that builds community. Toward this, the Spirit empowers and counsels us to faithfulness, including faithful communication.

PONDER: How have I experienced the Holy Spirit as part of my spirituality? How might I incorporate the fruits of the Spirit in my discernment of faithful communication?

PRAY: God of Wisdom and Counsel, your Holy Spirit is our faithful guide and continues to gather us to fullness of life in you. Our communication, essential to forming relationships, is faithful if it follows your Spirit. May we harvest the fruits of the Spirit and give them expression in the way we share ourselves with others. May these fruits nourish us to make a gift of self in love to those around us. We ask this in the name of Jesus Christ, by the power of the Spirit. Amen.

20

Silence in Heaven

(Revelation 7:9-14; 8:1-3, 5-6)

STATIO: Become still in body and mind. Take a minute to breathe and be aware of the moment.

LISTEN: What word or phrase stands out to you?

After this I had a vision of a great multitude, which no one could count, from every nation, race, people, and tongue. They stood before the throne and before the Lamb, wearing white robes and holding palm branches in their hands. They cried out in a loud voice:

> *"Salvation comes from our God, who is seated on the throne,*
> *and from the Lamb."*

All the angels stood around the throne and around the elders and the four living creatures. They prostrated themselves before the throne, worshiped God, and exclaimed:

> *"Amen. Blessing and glory, wisdom and thanksgiving,*
> *honor, power, and might*
> *be to our God forever and ever. Amen."*

Then one of the elders spoke up and said to me, "Who are these wearing white robes, and where did they come from?" I said to him, "My lord, you are the one who knows." He said to me, "These are the ones who have survived the time of great distress; they have washed their robes and made them white in the blood of the Lamb. . . ."

When he [the Lamb] broke open the seventh seal, there was silence in heaven for about half an hour. And I saw that the seven angels who stood before God were given seven trumpets.

Another angel came and stood at the altar, holding a gold censer. . . . Then the angel took the censer, filled it with burning coals from the altar, and hurled it down to the earth. There were peals of thunder, rumblings, flashes of lightning, and an earthquake.

The seven angels who were holding the seven trumpets prepared to blow them.

The Word of the Lord.

REFLECT: What does heaven sound like? In my imagination, it sounds like the first part of this reading: a great multitude of saints and angels praising God with songs and exclamations. A constant joyful praise. It is all the more striking, then, that this passage from Revelation goes on to note that there was "silence in heaven for about half an hour." Why does the great multitude fall silent?

In the context of this passage, the extended moment of silence marks a transition of sorts. Before the silence, we meet the great multitude in praise. And after the silence, a dramatic unfolding of events begins: angels take the prayers of the holy ones before the altar of God (8:4), then hurl down to earth burning coals from the same altar. Then, in the verses that follow, the angels blow their trumpets one by one and announce various tribulations to come before the fulfillment of God's final plan.

Why does heaven fall into silence? Here it is a sign of reverence, of awe, of holy fear before God. God is about to triumph once and for all and wipe away all that is not holy. Silence allows us to let that sink in, to ponder the mystery of God, the all-powerful sovereign one. As Zephaniah prophesies: "Silence in the presence of the Lord GOD! / for near is the day of the LORD" (1:7). Silence before God, even the silencing of our praise, allows God to be God—to be ever greater, to be outside of our boxes, to be Almighty and wholly other. Only in our silence can we seek further into Divine Mystery; only in silence do we make room for perceiving this expansive possibility and understanding more deeply who God is. Therefore, there must be silence in heaven. There must be moments when even the saints move more deeply into the inexhaustible mystery of God. This silence of heaven is a contemplative silence, a moment of unmediated intimacy and communion.

Esteeming silence is a consistent theme in the spiritual tradition. Silence is connected, for example, with humility and with virtuousness. Striving for silence with measured and intentional speech is in and of itself a spiritual discipline, while cursing and gossiping are sinful results of careless or excessive words. "Where words are many, sin is not wanting," warns Proverbs 10:19.

Silence is a spiritual discipline to lessen the occasion of sin, but it is also a spiritual end goal in itself. This is one of the mysteries of the spiritual life, since God gave us communication as a gift toward communion. When my children were born, it was eye-opening for me to realize how much human survival depends on communication. Infants arrive in the world utterly helpless, except for one powerful thing: their cry. The baby's cry is his or her God-given ability to engage the world: to call out for help, call out for companionship, call out to the other. In the beginning of their lives and for some time after, small children express their needs by their cry. In fact, so essential is crying to survival that when an infant or small child is silent for too long, it may signal that something is off or wrong. So powerful is a child's cry that a mother's brain registers it uniquely and profoundly.

Born with the God-given ability to cry out, we spend our lives cultivating the spiritual ability to keep silence. This too is a God-given instinct, even in digital culture. While we are still deepening our understanding of how to live faithfully in the digital world, we have often observed people taking social media breaks, turning off their profiles for Lent or Advent, for example, as part of their spiritual practice. In a more constructive way, we also have seen the proliferation of mindfulness-cultivating apps that seek to reintroduce intentional moments of silence into the digital experience. As a digital society, we have a shared sense that our world is busy and noisy, and that silence is a precious commodity. There is an innate spirituality in this desire for silence.

Pope Benedict XVI, reflecting on the value of silence in the digital world, has noted: "Silence is an integral act of communication; in its absence, words rich in content cannot exist."[1] Silence affords us the space for better interpersonal communication: I can better understand myself and listen to the other when there is silence.

Beyond the interpersonal, silence of course is also spiritual and signals growth in our spiritual life. Silence as a spiritual end goal yields a contemplative space, a kind of communion with God that no longer needs words to mediate it. In contemplative silence, one's encounter with God becomes especially intimate. *Lectio divina*, the holy reading of Scripture that monastics practice, is in fact a guided process to move from receiving and praying with God's Word to *wordlessly* contemplating it. Silence in this sense holds the experience of the Word. It is in silence that we prepare for the Word, and through the Word we are led back into silence.

Before we experience the silence of wordless contemplation, we practice silencing our words. Practicing silence makes room. By moderating or stopping our own words, we take on a posture that is open and seeks the mystery of others and the mystery of God. Here on earth, then, silence begins to move us into heavenly communion with God and with one another, as we make room to listen, to encounter, and to grow in relationship.

[1] Pope Benedict XVI, "Silence and Word: Path of Evangelization: Message of His Holiness Pope Benedict XVI for the 46th World Communications Day," January 24, 2012.

PONDER: How well do I keep silence? Do I struggle with moderating or restraining my own words? What helps me find stillness and inner solitude?

PRAY: Almighty God, you reveal yourself to us in Word and Spirit. Our silence is essential for us to receive your self-gift. Grant us the grace to be still and to come to know you ever more deeply. May we too be counted among the multitudes who praise you eternally, and who occasionally fall into silence, so as to enter more deeply into the communion of heaven. We ask this through Christ the Word, by the power of the Spirit. Amen.

Epilogue

Just a Beginning

On January 27, 2019, @Pontifex tweeted about Mary, Mother of God, as the first influencer: "With her 'yes,' Mary became the most influential woman in history. Without social networks, she became the first 'influencer': the 'influencer' of God. #Panama 2019."

The Liturgy of the Hours, the regular prayer pattern of the church, ends each day with Mary. Evening Prayer includes the recitation of her *Magnificat*, and Compline (Night Prayer) traditionally ends with a Marian hymn. It is fitting to finally turn these reflections on faith communication toward the example of Mary, both as an ending, but also as a way to begin in practice. This "ending with a beginning" is a gesture of hospitality, a "yes" to what is yet to come on our spiritual journeys.

Mary's word of "yes" begins an intimate new chapter with humankind's closeness to the Divine Word. As she receives the Incarnate Word within herself, a new dynamic of faith communication begins to unfold.

Mary is a fundamental model for faith communication in her intimate relationship with Word and Spirit. Just as Mary received both Word and Spirit by offering a gift of herself in love through her *fiat*, just as her body held the Word in listening and silence for the first months of the Incarnation, just as she offered the Incarnate Word to the world through her motherhood, just as she received in hospitality and care the grieving Beloved Disciple, and just as she prayerfully listened for the Spirit in the Upper Room, the school of Mary includes, in a profound way, the theology and practice of communication.

Mary continues to speak to digital culture, especially through her closeness to Word and Spirit, her conviction of speech (Luke 1:46-55), and her disposition to promote not herself but her Son (John 2:5). She is a woman of truth and tenderness, a woman of faith and questions, a woman of encounter and service, a woman of humility and strength.

It began for Mary with listening and with a "yes."

Mary, Mother of the Word and influencer of God, pray for us so we too may listen well and say "yes" faithfully to Word and Spirit in our digital culture. May we begin again with you to welcome the Word and be its faithful communicators. Amen.